Is the Common Man Too Common?

Is the Common Man

An Informal Survey of Our Cultural Resources

NORMAN : *University of Oklahoma Press*

Too Common?

and What We Are Doing about Them

JOSEPH WOOD KRUTCH

EDUARD C. LINDEMAN

ALISTAIR COOKE

GILBERT SELDES

ARTHUR MAYER

NORMAN COUSINS

HAROLD K. GUINZBURG

A. WHITNEY GRISWOLD

JOHN W. DODDS

C. W. DE KIEWIET

GEORGE F. KENNAN

D. W. BROGAN

Library of Congress Catalog Card Number: 54-5938

Copyright 1954 by the University of Oklahoma Press, Publishing Division of the University. Composed and printed at Norman, Oklahoma, U.S.A., by the University of Oklahoma Press.
First edition, May 1954. Second printing, October 1954.

Foreword

IN 1922 the late Harold Stearns edited a sensational symposium to which many intellectuals of that post-war generation contributed. Though it was called *Civilization in the United States,* many of the participants seemed to feel that there wasn't any, and part of the book's considerable success was due to the acerbity with which they said so.

The present volume, though more sharply focused, really considers the same subject from a different point of view. During the more than thirty years which have passed since the earlier symposium a distinctive American civilization has not only taken on a much more clearly defined outline but also given rise to the hope or fear that it prefigures the future, not only in the United States but in the world at large.

Few believe now, as it was fashionable to believe in the twenties, that a wise man will merely denounce the alleged crudities of a new barbarism and go elsewhere. For one thing there is no longer anywhere else to go;

"exile" is no longer very attractive. For another thing we see more clearly now than unfriendly critics saw then that the phenomenon with which we are faced is powerful and positive, not merely backward and crude. What they scorned as Americanism is certainly not something we shall soon get over. What distinguishes it is not merely youth, or inexperience, or rawness. It cannot be explained by such once fashionable terms as "Puritanism" or "Babbitry." For good or ill it is a much more portentous phenomenon than they supposed.

What really does distinguish it is simply the fact that for the first time in history material welfare and some sort of cultural opportunity are realities for the majority of citizens in a great nation. Suddenly the question has become not how this kind of democracy can be achieved but what its consequences are likely to be. Are they good; are they bad; or are they still potentially both? Can material and intellectual goods be made widely accessible without redefining what we mean by "the best"?

It is these questions or some aspect of them that each of the contributors considers. Their points of view as well as their special subjects are various, but they are alike in one respect. None uncritically accepts as good, or even ultimately good, every present manifestation of the world's first democratic civilization but neither does any one of them reject it as some contributors to the earlier symposium rejected the Americanism of their day. All recognize that the very instruments and techniques which have made mass wealth and mass culture possible make it also possible to manipulate, and vulgarize, and stultify the masses. All are concerned with both the question to what extent such vulgarization and stultification are actually taking place and the question to what extent we may, by taking thought, exploit the good and minimize the evil effects of the instruments and the ideals which are still molding the emerging American civilization.

Some deal specifically with some such phenomenon as the radio, the phonograph, or the mass-produced book. Others deal with such less tangible things as the standards of value which a mass culture tends to set up. But all recognize that this really is a new kind of world with problems as new as the techniques which have created it. Americans are sometimes accused of being more interested in going somewhere than in where they are going. The contributors to this symposium are not.

Joseph Wood Krutch

February 3, 1954
Tucson, Arizona

Contents

This book was edited with the assistance of William D. Patterson, associate publisher of *The Saturday Review,* who planned and co-ordinated the survey of the contemporary cultural scene in America contained in these pages.

Notes on the Contributors

D. W. BROGAN, the distinguished English social historian and professor of political science at Cambridge, is the author of a number of works on American life.

The author of *A Generation on Trial* and *Letters from America*, ALISTAIR COOKE has been chief correspondent in the United States for the *Manchester Guardian* since 1948.

Editor of the *Saturday Review* since 1942, NORMAN COUSINS is the author of *Who Speaks for Man?* a recent work pointing up the major issues of our civilization at mid-century. His other books include *Modern Man Is Obsolete, The Good Inheritance,* and *A Treasury of Democracy.*

A professor of English at Stanford University and director of the special program in humanities there, JOHN W. DODDS is the author of critical studies of Southerne and Thackeray.

A. WHITNEY GRISWOLD, who has been president of Yale

University since 1950, is the author of *The Far Eastern Policy of the U.S.*, *Farming and Democracy*, and *Essays on Education*.

Founder and president of the Viking Press, HAROLD K. GUINZBURG was a contributor to the recently published *Books and the Mass Market*.

A former ambassador to Russia, GEORGE F. KENNAN is now associated with the Institute for Advanced Study, Princeton, New Jersey.

President of the University of Rochester since 1953, C. W. DE KIEWIET has written a number of books on South Africa, including *A History of South Africa*.

JOSEPH WOOD KRUTCH, the noted drama critic, essayist, and author of many works on literary figures and trends, has been living in Tucson, Arizona, since his retirement from the Brander Mathews chair of dramatic literature at Columbia University.

A distinguished philosopher and a nationally respected leader in the field of adult education, the late EDUARD C. LINDEMAN was for many years a teacher in the New York School of Social Work of Columbia University.

The veteran motion picture executive ARTHUR MAYER is a contributor to many monthly publications and the author of a recent book of reminiscences, *Merely Colossal*.

GILBERT SELDES, who was associated with Columbia Broadcasting System for many years, is the author of *The Seven Lively Arts*, *The Great Audience*, and other books concerned with popular entertainment.

Is the Common Man Too Common?

I. Is the Common Man Too Common?

THE Age of the Common Man is not merely a phrase; it is also a fact. Already we are definitely entered upon it, and in all probability it is destined to continue for a long time, intensifying its characteristics as it develops in some of the directions which it has already begun to take.

Most people welcome the fact, but we have only begun to assess it or even to ask ourselves what choices are still open to us once the grand decision has been made, as by now it has. How common does the common man need to be? Does his dominance necessarily mean that the uncommon man will cease to be tolerated or that the world will become less suited to his needs, less favorable to the development of his talents than it now is? Will excellence be looked upon as in itself unworthy or "undemocratic"? Can we have an Age of the Common Man without making it an Age of the Common Denominator? Do any dangers lie ahead?

One way to approach these questions is, of course, to ask what has happened already, what changes in attitudes have demonstrably taken place, how the culture

3

of the first era of the Age of the Common Man differs from that which preceded it. What, in other words, is the culture of present-day America like, and are there aspects of it, directly traceable to the emphasis on the common man and his tastes, which are not wholly reassuring? And if there are, then to what extent are the defects corrigible, to what extent are they necessary consequences of the premises we have already accepted?

Unfortunately, but not surprisingly, there is no general agreement concerning the real nature of the situation at the present moment, though it does seem clear enough that most Americans judge both the present and the future a good deal more favorably than many observers from the Old World do. Thus, in his recent book *The Big Change,* Frederick Lewis Allen summed up very cogently the case for contemporary American culture. Hundreds of thousands read the selections of the book clubs; hundreds of thousands more attend concerts of serious music; millions listen to debates, symphonies, and operas on the radio. Never before in the history of the world has so large a portion of any population been so interested in and so alert to intellectual and artistic activities. Ours is the most cultured nation which ever existed.

Compare this with any one of the typical fulminations which proceed at regular intervals from European commentators and the result is both astonishing and disturbing. In Europe the prevalent opinion seems to be that this same civilization of ours constitutes a serious threat to the very existence of anything which can properly be called a culture.

We are told, in the first place, that for every American who does read the Book of the Month and attend a symphony concert there are a dozen who live in a vulgar dreamworld induced by a perpetual diet of soap operas, comic books, torch songs, and "B" movies. Moreover, the material prosperity and political power of this majority of sick barbarians enable them to become, as no cultural proletariat ever was before, a threat to every civilized minority. They rule the roost, and they are becoming less and less tolerant of anyone or anything superior to them.

In the second place—and perhaps even more importantly—the culture of even the minority is described as largely an imitation. It consumes but does not produce art. The best of the books it reads and the music it listens to is imported. Its members are really only parasites feeding upon European culture, and their sterility will in time kill it completely. Even their power to "appreciate" is essentially shallow—the result of superficial education, propaganda, advertisement, and a general pro-cultural hoop-la, all of which produce something very different indeed from that deep, personal, demanding passion for Truth and Beauty which has always been the dynamic force in the production of any genuine culture.

Now it is easy enough to dismiss this European view as merely the product of ignorance, prejudice, and envy. But it is dangerous to do so. To look candidly at the two pictures is to perceive something recognizable in both of them. Nobody really knows what the American phenomenon means or what it portends. And the reason is that it is actually something genuinely new. Whether

5

you call it the Dawn of the First Democratic Culture or call it the Triumph of Mediocrity, the fact remains that there is no obvious parallel in human history. Mr. Allen and those who agree with him are obviously right as far as they go. But the unique phenomenon which they describe can stand further analysis.

A college education for everybody and two cars in every garage are ideals not wholly unrelated. An even closer analogy can be drawn with the earlier, more modest ideal of universal literacy. America was the first country to teach nearly everybody to read. Whether we are quite aware of it or not, we are now embarked upon the pursuit of what is really an extension of the same ideal, namely, a minimum cultural literacy for all. There is vast difference between being barely able to spell out a newspaper and being able to read in the full sense of what the term implies. There is a similar and probably no greater difference between, say, being able to get something out of the movie *The Great Caruso* or the latest volume dispatched to the members of a book club by editors who have trained themselves to understand the limitations of their average subscriber, and a genuine grasp of either music or literature. The term "literacy" covers a large area whether we are using it in its limited sense or extending it to include what I have called "cultural literacy." A few generations ago we pointed with pride to the fact that most Americans "could read"; we now point with pride to the fact that an astonishing proportion of them "read serious books" or "listen to serious music," and in both cases we take satisfaction in a mass capacity which exists only if we define it in minimum terms. In

6

neither case does the phenomenon mean quite as much as those who celebrate it most enthusiastically sometimes seem to assume.

But, what, one may ask, is either disturbing or surprising about that? The minimum remains something more than any people as a whole ever before achieved. Is it likely that fewer people will read well just because a larger number can read a little? Is not, indeed, the opposite likely to be true? Is anything but good likely to come from the establishment of a broad base of even a minimum cultural literacy?

Any hesitation in answering "no" to the last question might seem at first sight to spring inevitably from nothing except arrogance, snobbishness, and a desire to preserve the privileges of an aristocracy. Yet a good many Europeans and an occasional American do seem inclined to take the negative position. The wide spread of our minimum culture does seem to them to constitute some sort of threat.

At least one fact or alleged fact they can cite as possible evidence on their side of the argument. So far, the number of recognized masterpieces produced by native-born Americans does seem disappointingly small when compared with the number of literate citizens we have produced. Is that because American art is inadequately recognized, or because we just haven't had time yet to mature? Or is it, perhaps, somehow connected—as some would say it is—with mass culture itself. Is the Good always the friend of the Best or is it sometimes and somehow the enemy? Is Excellence more likely to lose out to Mediocrity than it is to mere Ignorance or Nullity?

The line being taken in Europe today has a good deal in common with that of the twenties. To some extent indeed it may have been learned from our post-World War I intellectuals; the disdainful European conception of American society is a good deal like Mencken's Boobocracy. At the present moment, however, the current of opinion at home is running in the opposite direction, and it is no longer unusual for the confessed intellectual to defend the culture which his predecessor of a generation ago despised and rejected. But complacency has its dangers too, and it may be worth while to examine a little further what can be said in support of the European's thesis.

This, he hears us say, is the Age of the Common Man. But we as well as he are not quite certain what we mean by that. In so far as we mean only the age of universal opportunity, what was once called simply "the career open to talents," nothing but good could seem to come of it. But many people do, sometimes without being entirely aware of it, mean something more. When we make ourselves the champion of any particular group we almost inevitably begin to idealize that group. From defending the common man we pass on to exalting him, and we find ourselves beginning to imply not merely that he is as good as anybody else but that he is actually better. Instead of demanding only that the common man be given an opportunity to become as uncommon as possible, we make his commonness a virtue and, even in the case of candidates for high office, we sometimes praise them for being nearly indistinguishable from the average man in the street. Secretly, no doubt, we hope that they are somehow superior, but we feel at the same time that a kind of decency requires them to conceal the fact as completely as possible.

The logical extreme of this opinion would be the conviction that any deviation in either direction from the statistical average is unadmirable; even, to take a concrete example, that the ideal man or woman could best be represented, not by an artist's dream, but by a composite photograph of the entire population. And though few would explicitly acknowledge their acceptance of this extreme position, there is a very strong tendency to emphasize quantitative rather than qualitative standards in estimating achievement. We are, for instance, more inclined to boast how many Americans go to college than to ask how much the average college education amounts to; how many people read books rather than how good the books are; how many listen to the radio rather than how good what they hear really is.

Argue, as I myself have argued, that more can be learned about almost any subject from ten minutes with a printed page than from half an hour with even one of the better educational programs and you will be met with the reply: "Perhaps. But so many *more* people will listen to the radio." In a democracy quantity is important. But when the stress upon it becomes too nearly exclusive, then democracy itself threatens to lose its promise of moving on to higher levels. Thus the Good really can become the enemy of the Best if one insists upon exclusively quantitative standards.

Certainly one of the striking—some would say one of the inevitable—characteristics of our society is its penchant for making widely and easily accessible either substitutes for, or inferior versions of, a vast number of good things, like the vile substitute for bread available at any grocers. That bread can be come by without effort, and it may be true that fewer people are in want of bread of some kind than ever were in want of it in any society before. But that does not change the fact that it is a very inferior product.

Another and related tendency of this same society is its encouragement of passivity. A generation ago moralists viewed with alarm the popularity of "spectator sports": the fact that people gathered in stadia to watch others play games for them. But we have gone far beyond that and today the baseball fan who takes the trouble to make a journey to the Polo Grounds instead of watching the game on his TV set has almost earned the right to call himself an athlete. One wonders, sometimes, if the popularity of "discussion" programs does not mean very much the same thing; if most people have not now decided to let others hold remote conversations for them—as well as play remote games—even though the conversations are often no better than those they could hold for themselves.

As John Stuart Mill—certainly no antidemocrat— wrote a century ago: "Capacity for the nobler feeling is in most natures a very tender plant. . . . Men lose their high aspirations as they lose their intellectual tastes, because they have not time or opportunity for indulging them; and they addict themselves to inferior pleasures, not because they deliberately prefer them, but because they are either the only ones to which they have access, or the only ones which they are any longer capable of enjoying."

In the history books of the future this age of ours may come to be known as the Age of Statistics. In the biological and physical as well as the sociological sciences, statistics have become, as they never were before, the most important tool of investigation. But as every philosophical scientist knows, the conclusions drawn by a science depend to a considerable extent upon the tools used. And it is in the nature of statistics not only that they deal with quantity but that they emphasize the significance of averages and medians. What usually exists or usually happens establishes The Law, and The Law is soon thought of as identical with The Truth. In all the arts, nevertheless, it is the exceptional and unpredictable which really count. It is the excellent, not the average, which is really important. And there is, therefore, one aspect of the cultural condition of a civilization to which statistical study is curiously inappropriate.

No one, it may be said, needs to accept the inferior substitute or hold himself down to the average level. But simple and complete as that answer may seem to be, there are facts and forces which do tend to encourage an almost unconscious acceptance of mediocrity. One, of course, is that the inferior substitute—whether it be baker's bread or the movie show playing at the neighborhood house—is so readily accessible and so forced upon one's attention by all the arts of advertising as well as by the very way in which our lives have been organized. Another and more serious one is the tendency of the mass media to force out of the field every enterprise which is not based upon mass appeal. Whatever the reason may be, it is a generally recognized fact that it is becoming increasingly difficult, economically, to publish a book which is not a best seller or produce a play which is not a smash hit. More and more, therefore, artistic enterprise must be abandoned to the movies and to television where the mass audience is sufficient to defray the staggering cost.

Besides these economic reasons why the new media tend to concern themselves only with mass appeals, there is the additional technical reason why the two newest of such media tend to confine themselves to it. Since TV and radio channels are limited in number, all the arguments in favor of democracy as it is sometimes defined justify the existing fact that these channels should be used to communicate what the greatest number of people seem to want. That is the argument of the great broadcasting chains, and on the premise assumed it is a valid one.

The only mechanical instrument of communication which can make a reasonable case for the claim that it has actually served to increase the popularity of the thing communicated on its highest level of excellence is the phonograph, and it is significant that the phonograph is the only such device for communication which —especially since the invention of tape recording and LP—has found it economically feasible to cater to relatively small minorities. The fact that it does not cost much to produce a record may well have an incalculably great effect upon American musical taste.

What the question comes down to in the simplest possible terms is one of those which we asked at the very beginning of this discussion: Can we have an Age of the Common Man without having also an Age of the Common Denominator? That question has not been answered, probably cannot be convincingly answered, at the present moment. But it is a fateful question and the one with which this discussion is concerned.

One must not, of course, idealize the past to the extent of assuming that the best works were always, inevitably, and immediately the most popular. Two years ago James D. Hart's thorough and amusing *The Popular Book* (Oxford University Press) demonstrated conclusively that since colonial times there have always been absurd best sellers. The year that Hawthorne earned $144.09 royalties in six months was the year his own publisher paid Susan Warner $4,500 for the same period and another publisher sold 70,000 copies of one of Fanny Fern's several works.

Neither, I think, should it be supposed that any society ever has been or ever will be so organized as to favor exclusively the highest artistic excellence. As a system, aristocratic patronage is absurdly capricious; capitalistic democracy tends to favor vulgarity; socialism would probably favor official mediocrity. The question here is not whether contemporary America provides ideal conditions for cultural developments on the highest level, but whether it renders such development unusually difficult instead of making it, as the optimists insist, almost inevitable.

Of the unfavorable influences which I have mentioned, it seems to me that the most serious is the tendency to confuse the Common Denominator with a standard of excellence. The mechanical and economic facts which tend to give the purveyors of mediocrity a monopoly—highly developed in the case of radio and TV, probably growing in the publishing business—may possibly be changed by new developments, as they have already been changed in the case of the phonograph. But to confuse The Best with the most widely and the most generally acceptable is to reveal a spiritual confusion which is subtle and insidious as well as fundamental. It could easily nullify any solution of the mechanical and economic problems created by the age of mass production. How real and how general does this confusion seem actually to be?

More than one sociologist has recently pointed out that as technology integrates larger and larger populations into tighter and tighter groups the members of these groups tend inevitably to work, live, and recreate themselves in the same way and in accordance with the standardized patterns which the facilities provided for these various activities lay down. For ill as well as for good, "community living" becomes more and more nearly inevitable and individual temperament or taste finds less and less opportunity to express itself.

One result of this is that the natural tendency of the adolescent to practise a desperate conformity is prolonged into adult life and the grown man continues to want what his neighbors have, to do what his neighbors do, to enjoy what his neighbors enjoy. This is one of the things which the European may have in mind when he calls us a nation of adolescents, and commercial interests take advantage of our adolescent characteristics by stressing, through all sorts of publicity, the fact that this is the kind of cigarette most people smoke, the kind of breakfast food most people eat, and the torch singer or crooner most people like. The best-selling book is not only the easiest one to buy, but it is also the one we must read unless we are willing to be made to seem somehow inferior. What is most popular must be best. As a broadcast official recently said, to call the most popular radio programs vulgar is to call the American people vulgar. And that, he seemed to imply, was not merely nonsense but pretty close to treason. The voice of the people is the voice of God. God loves the common man. If the common man loves Bob Hope then God must love Bob Hope also. In musical taste as in everything else the common man is divine.

It is this logic which, unfortunately, the purveyors to the mass audience are very prone to follow. Undoubtedly, it leads them to the line of least resistance at the same time that it provides them with a smug excuse for both inanity and vulgarity. They are, they say, servants of the public and have no right to doubt that the people know not only what they want but what is good for them. The age of the common man has no place for any holier-than-thou attitude. It believes in government "by" as well as "for" the people. Totalitarianism is what you get when you accept the "for" but not the "by," and the attitude of, for example, the British Broadcasting Corporation, with its notorious Third Program, merely demonstrates that England has not yet learned what democracy really means.

15

No doubt the questions involved are too complicated to be discussed here. A few years ago, Charles A. Siepmann in his *Radio, Television, and Society* fully and impartially reported on both the policies and the arguments as they affect the media with which he was dealing. But at least one conclusion seems obvious. If there is any such thing as responsibility on the part of those most powerful and best informed towards those whose appetites they feed, then no provider of movies or records or television programs may escape the minimal duty of giving his public the best rather than the worst it will stand for. Mr. Mencken once declared that no one had ever gone bankrupt by underestimating the taste of the American public, but there is an increasing tendency to believe that, by dint of long trying, certain commercial exploiters of the mass media have succeeded only too well in underestimating it considerably.

What is obviously called for is a public opinion less ready than it now is to excuse the failure to meet even minimal responsibilities; but that public opinion is not likely to arise unless those responsible for public thinking play their own parts, and there is a tendency for them to yield rather than protest. Unfortunately, the fanatical exaltation of the common denominator has been taken up not only by the common man himself and by those who hope to profit by his exploitation but also and increasingly by those who are supposed to be educators and intellectual leaders. Instead of asking "What would a good education consist of?" many professors of education are asking "What do most college students want?"; instead of asking "What books are wisest and best and most beautiful?" they conduct polls to determine which the largest number of students have read with least pain. Examination papers are marked, not in accordance with any fixed standard, but in accordance with a usual level of achievement; the amount of work required is fixed by the amount the average student does; even the words with which the average student is not familiar are edited out of the books he is given to read. How, granted such methods, is it other than inevitable both that the average will seldom be exceeded and that the average itself will gradually drop?

As David Reisman and his collaborators pointed out two years ago in their brilliant analysis called *The Lonely Crowd* (Yale University Press), the ideal now persistently held before the American citizen from the moment he enters kindergarten to the time when he is buried under the auspices of a recognized funeral parlor is a kind of conformity more or less disguised under the term "adjustment." "Normality" has almost completely replaced "Excellence" as an ideal. It has also rendered all but obsolescent such terms as "Righteousness," "Integrity," and "Truth." The question is no longer how a boy ought to behave but how most boys do behave; not how honest a man ought to be but how honest men usually are. Even the Robber Baron, who represented an evil manifestation of the determination to excel, gives way to the moneymaker who wants only to be rich according to the accepted standards of his group. Or, as Mr. Reisman sums it up, the American who used to be conspicuously "innerdirected" is now conspicuously "outerdirected."

According to the anthropologists, many primitive societies are based almost exclusively upon the idea of conformity and generate what are, in the anthropologist's meaning of the term, remarkable cultures. It may, of course, be argued that America and the whole world which follows in America's wake is evolving in the direction of this kind of culture. But if by "culture" we mean something more narrowly defined, if we mean a culture which is continuous with that of the Western world since the Renaissance, then it is my contention that it cannot flourish where the stress is as nearly exclusively as it threatens to become upon "adjustment," "normality," or any of the other concepts which, in the end, come down to mean that the Common Denominator is identical with the Ideal. Especially, it cannot flourish under these conditions if the result which they tend to produce is intensified by the fact that ingenious methods of mass production and mass propaganda help impose upon all the tyranny of the average.

Salvation, if salvation is possible, may be made so by technological developments like those in the phonograph industry which tend to break monopoly and permit the individual to assert his preferences and his tastes. But the possible will not become the actual if in the meantime the desire for excellence has been lost and those who should be leaders have willingly become followers instead. If the Age of the Common Man is not to become the Age of the Common Denominator rather than what it was originally intended to be—namely an age in which every man had the opportunity to become as superior as he could—then the cultural as well as the political rights of minorities must somehow be acknowledged. There is not really anything undemocratic about either the desire for, or the recognition of, excellence. To prove that ours is the most cultured nation which ever existed will constitute only a barren victory if we must, to prove our point, use nothing but quantitative standards and reconcile ourselves to the common denominator as a measure of excellence.

One might sum up the situation in a series of propositions. (1) The Age of the Common Man has begun. (2) Despite all the gains that it may legitimately claim, they are threatened by those confusions which arise when the common denominator is consciously or unconsciously allowed to function as a standard of excellence. (3) The dominance of mass media almost exclusively under the control of those who are little concerned with anything except immediate financial gain does tend to debase taste. (4) Ultimate responsibility for the future rests with the thinkers and the educators whose most important social task at the moment is to define democratic culture in some fashion which will both reserve a place for uncommon excellence and, even in connection with the largest masses, emphasize the highest rather than the lowest common denominator.

2. The Common Man as Reader

FISHER AMES liked to compare democracy with a raft. The raft, he said, does not sink, but those who ride it are continually in danger of getting their feet wet. Among the many meanings which might be attached to this simile is the notion that every move in a democratic direction involves a risk. Our founding fathers, for example, thought it might be dangerous to permit any but property-owners to vote. This risk was finally taken, and we have now achieved universal suffrage. In the early days of the Republic it was thought by many that education should remain a privilege of the elite. Nevertheless, this risk was also taken, and we now enjoy free public education for everyone.

Very few Americans, I assume, would now advocate a return to limited suffrage and restricted education. Is this democratic urge destined to extend its inclusiveness indefinitely? Are there no limits? Is there to be no aristocracy in any sphere? In the realm of culture, for example? Are we to assume that books and art and music are all to be democratized, made available to the masses? If so, what risk is involved?

Affirmative answers to these questions are now emerging. Certainly, in the realm of books we now have some reliable evidence of the consequences of democratization. Through the instrumentality of science, technology, and business enterprise, that irresistible trinity of resources which accounts for the dynamic quality of our civilization, books have become available to the mass market. Publication of low-priced, paper-covered books, mostly reprints which first appeared in expensive hard covers, has produced results which may be described only by the use of superlatives.

In 1941 American readers bought 231,000,000 volumes in paper-bound covers. The boom in pocket-sized books began in 1939 and during that year the total sales amounted to only 3,000,000. Readers pay twenty-five, thirty-five, or fifty cents for each book, and in 1951 they expended $63,000,000 for this purpose. These startling totals continue to be exceeded each year.

Two hundred millions of anything represents an ample sampling, and it should now be feasible to draw some qualitative conclusions. Educators will most certainly be eager to learn what Americans will read when books become readily available. Indeed, this question has already become sufficiently important to become the object of inquiry of a special committee of Congress! The danger involved in the democratization of book distribution on a mass scale is that cheapness of price may become an index of cheapness of taste. There is no worry about the discriminating reader who takes pains to se-

21

lect his books from the stacks of his free public library, nor of the reader who can afford to buy the books he wants at his local book shop. The question of taste arises when prospective readers, in numbers hitherto unsuspected, buy their books at the corner drugstore, the tobacco shop, or a department store—a transaction which is inexpensive and convenient. There are some who seem to believe that inexpensive books will bring about a universal vulgarization of taste. A few even go so far as to believe "there ought to be a law," that some omnipotent government agency should censor the publishing business and thus determine in advance the character of books which Americans may be permitted to buy and read. These extremists, apparently unaware of the fact that experience demonstrates that censorship invariably exacerbates the evil it is intended to abate, believe that the judgment of the people is not to be trusted. They wish to get off the "raft" and find a completely reliable craft whose officers will guarantee that no one will henceforth get "his feet wet." These are the frightened ones who have lost faith in democracy because they have never really believed it to be an experiment in learning through experience, basically an educational enterprise in which freedom of choice is the principal ingredient, in which it is assumed that the arts of self-government can be learned only through the exercise of governing one's self.

All of this was said with eloquence in an almost forgotten book of wisdom written long ago by the late David Starr Jordan in *The Voice of the Scholar*. "It is," he wrote, "unfortunately, one of the conditions of de-

mocracy that wisdom and its counterfeit go along together side by side. There can be no tag or label to mark
one from the other, nor would the people need them if
there were. But all this is well. It is better for men to
choose the voice of wisdom for themselves rather than
to have it infallibly pointed out by government. For the
seat of wisdom is in the individual soul and it grows
through individual effort." Yes, but what of the risks?
Are there not critical moments in history when the voice
of the people goes wrong, when the authoritative strong
leader is necessary? Or, returning to our immediate preoccupation, namely cheap books, is it not likely to be
true that cheapness of price will automatically induce
cheapness of taste?

What is revealed by the evidence? Analysis of the
sales of inexpensive, paper-bound books during the last
decade and a half reveals first of all the realistic fact that
American readers may be arranged on a graded scale in
which the lowest level represents those who display a
vulgar taste and the highest an extraordinary quality of
discernment. In other words, we are a variable people
with tastes which range from execrable to excellent. The
evidence also appears to demonstrate that our tastes as
made manifest in our free choice of reading matter are
natural reflections of our culture and our experience as
a people. Americans, for example, buy so-called "Westerns" in large numbers. One reprint publishing company
furnishes at least one per month. The internal pattern
or plot of these Western stories in which cowboys, officers of the law, villains, and beautiful but brave young
women play their respective roles is so familiar that read-

ers know in advance what the outcome will be. Why, then, do they continue—with a few praiseworthy exceptions on a higher and more sophisticated level—to repeat this experience? (Incidentally, this same question applies to Western movies, which continue to be the safest investment in that precarious industry which also caters to a wide range of tastes.) The answer is incredibly simple. We read Westerns because the frontier is a cherished element in our experience as a people. Every American is a potential pioneer. In every American there lies dormant the feeling that he too might play the part of hero. Every American is a latent out-of-door person. Commercial rodeos attract their largest audiences in the arenas of metropolitan centers. In short, the West is "in our blood," and writers who can evoke these latencies are responding to a taste which is typically American.

It is also a symbol of escape from reality? Is there a mass audience for Westerns because the romantic West no longer exists? Are we, in other words, perpetuating a fantasy. Is this type of reading an indication that our lives have now become drab and unexciting and that hence we must find some compensation in an imaginary West where "men are men," where some are plainly good and others blatantly bad, and where virtue always triumphs in the end? Perhaps so, but who assumes that life anywhere is so perfect as not to require compensations? Is it not in one sense the principal function of fiction of any type to furnish compensation? The "classic" Westerns are nothing more than oversimplified novels. They permit the reader to identify himself with uncomplicated virtue.

But the would-be censors are not too much troubled over the fact that hundreds of thousands of American readers buy reprint Westerns. Their chief complaint is focused upon sex and crime (violence) and the interplay between these two aspects of contemporary life. Sex is a haunting specter in the American experience. And violence is so much of an "attraction" that it dominates the pages of our newspapers. Inexpensive books dealing with these two phases of our lives enjoy a mass consumption, and this should have been anticipated. Indeed, magazine publishers and advertisers of all varieties had already demonstrated the efficacy of "selling" through the exploitation of sex. There is even a newspaper columnist whose vogue rests upon the discovery that females with partially exposed or exaggerated mammillary glands are objects of intense interest on the part of American readers. Why this is so must be left to psychiatrists. What would happen if it was thought to be too great a risk to permit American readers to satisfy this taste and attempts were made to repress it? If past experiences with suppression are to be trusted, we know what would happen: the "appetite" would increase and its pathological manifestations would become more prominent. If, in other words, it is assumed that the mass sales of books dealing with sex and crime symbolize something vulgar in the American character, what would be the educator's strategy if he believed it desirable and feasible to alter or modify this taste? I shall postpone my answer to this question until two other manifestations of American literary taste are dealt with.

Publication of inexpensive paper-bound books has

revealed a considerable market for so-called science-fiction. The juxtaposition of these two words, or rather their conjunction, seems at first glance to constitute a paradox. Science is concerned with facts whereas fiction typifies life's romantic element. Fiction, even when it is naturalistic in temper and method, does not obey the strict rules of scientific evidence. Why do Americans have a taste for conjoining the facts of science and the most fantastic imaginings of romanticists? Here again the answer when sought in cultural contexts is relatively simple. We have never accepted the scientific view of our universe. We seek from science more gadgets, not a *Weltanschauung.* Rocket ships, atomic bombs, and automobiles are the romantic end-products of the scientific mind. So long as we can foresee more of such "miracles" emanating from scientific research, just so long are we protected from the disturbing necessity of deserting some of our cherished myths. Who is to say when these myths, these unscientific views of life are no longer capable of serving a useful compensatory purpose? In one sense the taste for science-fiction may be regarded as lack of maturity. On the other hand, it may be explained as a new form of transcendentalism, a way of viewing the universe which utilizes facts in order to transcend the merely factual. In any case, there it is. Americans like science-fiction, and when they are free to choose they will buy such books in large quantities.

Chronic deplorers, critics of American literary tastes, seem to believe that mass sales of mystery stories is a sign of low taste. Mystery or detective stories no longer represent a clear-cut classification. The sex motif has become so prominent in some such books that it tends in many cases to overshadow the criminal plot. But the mystery story is still essentially a form of literature in which the principal focus of interest is the fact that some unknown person has committed a crime and the reader is kept in suspense until the guilty person is made known, usually in the last chapter, through the subtle reasoning power of a detective. Multiple variations of this theme have been attempted by modern writers, but the outcome is always the same. And yet addicts of detective stories purchase millions of such books annually. I have heard of readers who read at least one per week. Why? In this instance the cultural explanation is not so simple. Steady readers of mystery stories offer a rationalized explanation which is almost wholly compensatory in meaning. They say they read mysteries because it takes them "out of this world." It releases them from the strains and stresses of contemporary life. It presents them with problems which they know in advance will be resolved but for the solution of which they bear no responsibility. The real world with its real problems thus becomes more bearable.

This interpretation may be accepted since all fictional literature performs a similar function, but why are Americans haunted particularly by crime? Ours is perhaps the most legalistic of all modern civilizations. We have agreed to give the courts a higher authority than either the legislative or executive branches of government. A Congressional committee, after making a study of delinquency, crime, and corruption, arrives at recommendations which are all in essence proposals to pass more laws, thus illustrating again our almost pathetic faith in the Law as an instrument for improving human behavior.

Our lives are thus embedded in legalism, but at the same time most Americans bear a resentment against those legal institutions which attempt to regulate their behavior. They are nevertheless tormented by an antithetical sentiment, namely, the feeling that specific guilt should be revealed and punished.

No one who seriously studies American culture will, I believe, deny that we are as a people peculiarly involved in delinquency, crime, and corruption. Nor will such a student be surprised if he is told that books dealing with these and related topics will be widely read when made accessible to a mass market.

We have now taken a cursory look at the four types of books which make up a large proportion of the sales of inexpensive reprints: Westerns, sex romances, science-fiction, and mysteries. These are the principal categories, and it is the mass sale of books in these classifications which forms the economic base of the reprint publishing business. Inexpensive books effectively distributed have demonstrated that these books are indicative of American taste. Literary taste is in one sense a reflection of cultural experience and cultural value. In another sense it reflects deep-seated cultural needs. Consequently, before the tastes of a people are condemned, before the critic resorts to moral judgments, he should take a realistic look at the cultural matrix from which taste emerges. Are these books true reflections of basic ingredients in our civilization? If so, whoever makes such books available to the mass market is making a valid response to human need.

Although it is unmistakably true that skill and craftsmanship in the writing of books in these categories has immeasurably improved since the rise in mass production, it is also true that if American taste were appraised solely on this index it would leave most of us, especially educators, in a despondent mood. But we need not become despondent, because the democratization of book publishing has also demonstrated another fact of far greater importance. We now know that millions of American readers are hungry for the best. Reprint publishers have uncovered a latent market for the very best in world literature, a market so large and so responsive as to restore one's faith in democracy. Who would have dreamed a decade ago that a scholarly book on anthropology (Ruth Benedict's *Patterns of Culture*) would, when made easily available at a low price, produce a buying public of half a million readers? Who would have suspected that millions of American readers wanted to read Shakespeare, Emerson, Whitehead, Sherwood, Dewey, Zola, Commager, Huxley, to mention only a few of the authors whose works have now become available! The record is almost incredible. There is a genuine taste for philosophy, science, religion, belles-lettres, and fiction of the highest order.

All of which brings us to the educator's responsibility. How is taste in reading to be improved? Unless democracy itself disintegrates, we must assume that there will be a further extension of freedom of choice. More people will be enabled to express their needs and fulfill their wants. This, as we have already pointed out, involves a risk. They may want more of the wrong things. The mere quantitative spread of fulfillment, if unaccompanied by an elevation of taste, may result in universal vulgarization. Some critics are afraid to take this risk. They want an authority, an elite, to prescribe the people's wants and desires. Others seem to believe that repression, suppression, and condemnation will effectively alter people's habits.

I reject both proposals. The only effective way of getting rid of a bad habit is to supplant it with a better one. Fortunately, most of our more important reprint publishers are aware of this psychological principle and are constantly reaching out for quality material. A few do not, and these have unhappily given the business a dubious reputation. But the movement is definitely upward. Greater quantities of quality books are reprinted year by year. Reprint publishers now vie with each other in a fierce competition for the republishing rights of books with a classical status. Reputable authors who only a few years ago withheld their books from the mass market are now eager to have their best works appear in paper covers. As usually happens when democracy is extended, the people will respond by allowing their better impulses a fuller sway. The democratic "revolution" in publishing has become another graphic illustration of the efficacy of the democratic faith.

3. The Press and Cultural Democracy

T HE "common man" is the pet abstraction of the post-
war decade, as the "little man" was of the one before
it. They are both patronizing terms and, we may be sure,
were not invented by the people they were meant to
describe. Joseph Mitchell once dedicated a book to "the
little man, who is bigger than you whoever you are." I
wish somebody would do the same for the common man
and free him from the inhuman attributions of a saintly,
undemanding plumber biding his time. The common
man, if he could ever be found, would probably turn out
to be as cagey, good-natured, and egotistical as any reader of the *Saturday Review*.

So far as I can see, the "common man" was a necessary invention of the twentieth-century tyrants. It is a
flattering narcissistic image imposed on every wage earn-
er who for one reason or another is not earning enough.
It should be a warning to us that in at least three countries in the 1920's there were enough of him hungry and
hopeless to enable Hitler, Mussolini, and Stalin to con-

vince the average German he was a have-not, the average Italian that he was a Roman robbed of his birthright, the average Russian that he was the archetype of the modern man stunted in his growth by the luxury of the Imperial court. In Britain the only collection of common men I ever saw who eagerly embraced the title was the drooling rabble that followed Oswald Mosley; and in this country the delegates to Henry Wallace's 1948 convention: a nondescript press-gang of old fashioned radicals, embittered folk-singers, bewildered farmers, self-conscious liberals, parlor pinks, Greenwich Village *femmes fatales,* Sunday School superintendents, and reformed-calendar fanatics. There is a warning in the demonstrable fact that this feverish and motley crew was manipulated with ridiculous ease by an élite corps of Communists while the leader grew hoarse with declarations of independence and promises of freedom. The "common man" theme is a dangerous tune for Americans to play, for we are prone to sentimentalize the abstract average citizen (one in two of him doesn't vote) especially in all the regions of the country we don't know at first hand. And the appeal to his horse-sense, decency, energy, and "right" to enjoy everything is a temptation which, if we keep insisting on it, some smart demagogue one of these days will decide to monopolize.

On, come on, I can hear the sociologist and the editorial writer scold, you know what we mean. Well, I don't, but I will do my best. I take it that what is agitating the gentlemen who devised this symposium is the promise or threat of industrial democracy, and the effect of it on various cultural institutions which were invented by quite different societies. How does the prospect of swift world communications, universal primary education, and a vote for everyone, affect the future of the daily newspaper?

There was a time, we are told, when a gentleman retired to his study to read the London *Times* with an open atlas at his elbow. This day is long gone and for much the same reason that at least two of the nouns in that first sentence are today faintly offensive: a "gentleman" is a dying ideal, except on the understanding that every American boy can get to be one; and a "study" is in modern real estate a euphemism for a bar or has already been converted into a television "nook." In short, the idea of a good newspaper as a daily adjunct to the library of a professional man—a private bulletin written for the businessman, the parson, the politician, the scholar by a staff of confidential clerks—is on its death bed along with all other manifestations of minority culture in a mass civilization.

This opposition between the minority and the mass may be purely presumptive, but we seem to assume these days that it is a law of nature, and it is now as powerful a prejudice as the late nineteenth-century belief that the sciences and the arts were somehow natural enemies and that a man who knew the pollen-grain count of a daffodil was thereby disqualified from appreciating Wordsworth's poem. The Western mind has for several centuries at least contained a whole system of opposites which seem naïve and odd only to a Persian or a student of primitive languages. The minority versus the mass is only the latest form of such old antinomies as the Philistine versus the chosen people, the aristocrat versus the plutocrat, the Harvard man versus the rest. The people to blame for this pat, and as we today believe snobbish, doctrine are not the prosperous upper-middleclass Victorians but the Greeks, with their fundamental belief that some people were born to labor and some few to feel, to think, to practice and enjoy the fine arts. It is from this parent culture, which 400 years of Western education has systematically idolized, that we inherit the suspicion we all publicly deny that the common man must be isolated from his fellows in order to become an uncommon man. The Greeks never confused the value of the uncommon man, and the rarity of excellence, with the merely political doctrine that some rights belong equally to all men.

The first attempts in the English-speaking world to found a press were in England in the late sixteenth century: they were broadsides and comic strips, illustrating such things as the strictly British view of what happened to the Armada. There was even an enterprising Cockney, one Nathaniel Butter, who as early as 1605, before there were any newspapers at all in England, went up to Yorkshire and attended a couple of murder trials and, acting on the hunch that people had a vast and consuming interest in murder, got out some little tabloids which sold like hot-cakes. But they were for the instruction of the *hoi polloi,* a dangerous novelty, and were suppressed. From their earliest days, English newspapers required a royal license, and the first professional journalists were a private variation on what we should today call the press officer. Their job was not to inform the public but to keep their employers, usually a noble lord busy hunting or playing faro, in touch with what was happening abroad. The first American journalist was a confidence man of the same stripe. He was a sort of colonial Kiplinger who sent a regular newsletter to his "good and gracious lord" to give him the news of the Virginia colony. A Bostonian did the same for the New England governors and was little more than a private informer; for the burden of his letters was an account of how the true faith was developing in Boston, together with a list of dangerous dissenters known to be at large on the public highways. This was the origin of the paper which assumes it is informing an educated reader. Put this way, it sounds like an oddity, but in fact it is the type of the only newspapers we boast about.

This is a conception not very far removed from the tradition of patronage and, indeed, those papers that still try to maintain it depend for their survival on a reserve of private wealth, a trust agreement, an income from some unrelated business, or some other form of disguised subsidy. The *New York Times* could not possibly maintain its lavish foreign bureaus without its tedious bulk of profitable advertising copy. The only New York newspaper that tried to shuck off the necessary evil of advertising was kept alive by strong injections of money derived from a department store fortune; and when the Leftist line that it marketed went out of fashion, the paper went out of business. The London *News Chronicle* is a liberal paper owned and similarly reimbursed by the healthiest of English Quaker fortunes. The *Manchester Guardian,* a paper that all the world respected

35

but not to the extent of enough people buying it, was almost killed off by the depression. Long before 1929, its aging editor, C. P. Scott, was pondering the necessarily precarious future of an independent newspaper owned, in the strong nineteenth-century tradition, by one family. And it may be worth a retrospective glance at the period in the late nineteenth century when the omens first appeared which subsequently liquidated so many independent papers and now, in an age of mass communication, threaten to drown the survivors.

In the middle nineteenth century there were started, in the provinces of England and Scotland, a handful of papers by men who had a very distinct idea of what a newspaper ought to be. Papers like the *Yorkshire Post,* the *Sheffield Telegraph,* the *Birmingham Post,* the *Manchester Guardian* were each the inspiration and property of one man. They all assumed that a paper should be owned by one family, that it should be a messenger of news to the merchant class and a guide to the good life for everybody else. It sounds like a smug conception of public service but the evidence cannot be denied that the best in English journalism to this day is a by-product of this tradition of individualism which now seems certain to die.

It was a tradition developed in the latter half of the nineteenth century for some simple and realistic reasons. Not until the 1860's did Parliament finally abolish the heavy load of taxes that hampered any regular effort to report the news domestic and foreign: a stamp tax, a tax on paper, a tax on the right to print news from London, to report the doings of the House of Commons. The first big threat to the local monopoly, and the personal quality, of these papers was the roaring success of the news agencies. Julius Reuter, who had started with pigeons, was soon laying cables. It took money to organize these overseas services, it took money to subscribe to them, but by the 1880's the rewards were apparent in a daily display of seeming omniscience from all the capitals of Europe. The independent papers did not want to print what other papers could buy. Their pride was in their special correspondents. But they could not, and still cannot, afford to start up bureaus in all the places that Mr. Reuter had a man on tap. The news agency paved the way for a novel and shattering view of a newspaper, not as a public service but as a profitable industry. It needed only the discovery of wood pulp, around the turn of the century, to make the independent rag paper a struggling anachronism.

The proper formula had now been isolated: Lord Northcliffe + wood pulp = a mass circulation paper. The year after the discovery of wood pulp, the first daily penny paper in England trebled its circulation. In 1904 the *Daily Mail* sold one million copies a day. Local papers were absorbed into chains or succumbed like flies in December. "Absorption, amalgamations, and alliances": to Lord Northcliffe this was the obvious law of survival. "Combination," he said in 1913, "has been the chief characteristic of industry all over the world and the press could not remain outside this tendency."

Pondering all this in the much-celebrated autumn of his life, C. P. Scott might have been content to picture himself as the last of a noble line of martyrs. Instead, on the hundredth anniversary of the *Guardian* in 1921, when he himself was seventy-five, he wrote: "A newspaper has two sides to it. It is a business, like any other, and has to pay in the material sense in order to live. But it is much more than a business; it is an institution; it reflects and it influences the life of a whole community; it may affect even wider destinies. It is, in its way, an instrument of government . . . a newspaper is of necessity something of a monopoly, but its first duty is to shun the temptations of a monopoly." He had long ago felt the chill of the east wind. He saved money at every turn. He bicycled to work and brought his lunch in a paper bag. (This was simply North-of-England thrift, but it was a useful ally.) Although he was the paper's sole proprietor, he took no profits and assigned himself a fixed annual salary which could conceivably keep our own press lords in one chauffeur. He built up the reserves of the paper and purchased the *Manchester Evening News,* a popular evening paper, as a bulwark against hard times. And so it has been ever since. He then divested himself and his family of all financial interest in the paper. When he died his son legalized this asceticism and set up a trust, which assures that no one can take any dividends from the paper and that every penny of profit is ploughed back into its operation.

I have written at length about the *Guardian* simply because it is the paper I know best, because it does not pretend to compete with the mass circulation paper, and because it resolved in an interesting way the conflict between public service and the need to survive. The more serious American papers also have to try and protect themselves against successful "amalgamations and alliances." Sometimes they can claim a benefit from American geography. Whereas every native of Manchester, Sheffield, or Glasgow can have any or all of the big London dailies on his doorstep every morning, the citizens of Louisville or Salt Lake City are more dependent for their general news on the local paper. And where in such cities one paper is well established, there is less need to fear the competition of the *New York Daily News* or the *Chicago Tribune*. Even so, the American publisher, in any city, can hardly afford Scott's luxury of maintaining the quality and independence of his paper in the knowledge that his circulation is the lowest of three local papers. Circulation has been a nagging spur to all American papers, and the circulation war was an American phenomenon sixty years before the popular London dailies began to fight each other for the readership of every English town and hamlet.

The American nineteenth-century story has some fascinating strains of its own, and I can only list them here. The first daily newspaper in the United States had more advertising than news. The "leg-man," a sleuth still almost unknown in English newspapers, was born full-grown in the ingenious person of Henry Ingram Blake, who used to sail down the harbor and pick up the European dispatches from incoming ships and beat his competitors by half a day. The Baltimore *Sun* established a pony express. Even by the mid-nineteenth century, the *big* newspaper was the normal thing, which may reflect less the American appetite for news than the alertness of advertisers in getting in on the ground floor. As early as the 1840's there was a running fight between the developing tabloids and the big respectable papers. The serious papers called their competitors "the penny trash" and the "penny trash" referred back to our "bed-quilt contemporaries." There is also in the American experience the important conception of the newspaper proprietor as a crusader.

But in spite of all these instructive differences the plight of the independent paper, whether metropolitan or rural, is today much the same in both countries. In both countries there are less newspapers than there used to be (in 1909 there were 2,600 in the United States, today there are about 1,700) and there is less and less variety, or recognizable local comment, in the newspapers that exist. Probably not more than one American in, say, seventy or eighty has much of a choice in his own town of buying two sides of the news. This starving-out of local opinion is often explained away by saying that it is much easier now for a local paper to buy a great variety of comment from the syndicates, and that the exchange is a good bargain. But it seems to me, in traveling across the country, that the press becomes less and less of an index to regional character and that what takes its place is an artificial debate, packaged in New York, which has the effect of obliterating or discouraging independent thinking. Good or bad, what the columnists provide is a wild variety of unproved assertion, which could be something quite different from freedom of the press.

These are familiar lamentations, but they are none the less real. We gasp with pity at the thought of the worker in Minsk, the farmer in the Ukraine, both reading the same editorial, mimeographed by *Pravda* in Moscow for the instruction of European and Mongoloid Russians alike. Yet in our own country we seem to be approaching the day when the steel worker in Gary, Indiana, and the date-farmer in Indio, California, will buy their local paper and get their foreign news from the same agency man in Berlin or Washington, and read the same columns written by the same men in New York or Washington. If you go down to Times Square, or that block-long newsstand off Hollywood Boulevard, you can, on an investment of about three dollars in fifty-odd American newspapers, discover that the day is nearly here.

I fear, myself, that there is at least one generation of Americans growing up that not only does not have much respect for diversity of opinion but doesn't know what it is. It is only a step to believing that what is strange or unreported by fifty newspapers is somehow mischievous or "un-American." Once every man reads the same things as his neighbor, and thinks the same thoughts, the common man is here with a vengeance; that is to say, the mass bigot. I believe the British are not so far along this road as the Americans, but only because the big newspaper monopolies must, in a tiny country, do battle in all the same places. The British, too, are still preserved from conformity by the tenacity of such old habits as a tolerance for eccentrics and a mania for privacy.

I would say that because of this shrinking choice and because of the entailed indifference to the virtue of diversity, American newspapers are unrepresentative of the whole community and are becoming even more so.

If I seem to be harping away at the value of variety, tolerance, and diversity it is because, maybe, I suffer from the prejudice of other immigrants that the best qualities of America are rooted in these values. If they are to last, they should certainly be independent of class, income, region, or faith, and any community that denies them is certainly paying a high price for peace and comfort.

What is the answer? I frankly don't know, but not enough people will want to seek it until more people feel moved to ask the question. It is an obviously unhealthy thing, and I should have thought very "un-American," to have so many cities where there is only one newspaper, of a pronounced political bent, or where the morning and evening newspaper are owned by the same company. Is it too much to suggest that the Sherman Act might have a wide field of application here? Of course, no amount of reforming legislation can cure the newspaper publisher of his minimum responsibilities in a technological age: the pressing competition of radio and television; the need for a highly efficient modern plant; a dependable pool of advertising revenue; the inescapable fact that he must employ a crew of union labor that is organized on the tacit understanding that he is not on their side; his vested interest in low tax rates. He must often feel that the "common man" is a faceless army organized against him; and that they would be the last people to welcome the competition of another paper— a choice of conclusions.

Yet, unless the newspaper is to become merely another more or less profitable business, it cannot ignore Scott's dictum: "It is in its way, though it tries not to be so, an instrument of government. It plays on the minds and consciences of men. It may educate, stimulate, assist, amuse, or it may do the opposite. It has therefore, a moral as well as a material existence, and its character and influence are in the main determined by the balance of these two forces." A common man who is unaware of this balance, and is indifferent to striking it, is something very common indeed. (I am thinking of the publisher, not his readers. In fact, it seems to me that it is the publisher who has gotten way beyond himself and exceeded his proper function by becoming the head and dictator of the newspaper hierarchy. It is the editor who should be the brains and conscience of the paper. The intrusion of the publisher on editorial policy, wherever it occurs, produces an imbalance of Scott's "two forces" which deranges the proper function of a newspaper and makes it primarily a business or an annex of partisan political power.)

If our newspapers can remain diverse enough, and cherish even a cantankerous variety of opinion based on the same facts, then there is a good chance that we shall have the freedom to get up off our knees in the year 2000 and feel that our enforced devotion to the century of the common man has not been, after all, a blind surrender of human individuality to the lowest common denominator. In my opinion we are, however, beginning to succumb to this religion and will leave ourselves perilously open to the man or government that could exploit it, if newspapers—as an example—are forced to sacrifice to such secondary and ruinous aims as building a lucrative business, or purchasing a local pulpit, their first purpose:

43

which is the unhampered dissemination of any news a reporter can smell out, and the printing of the widest variety of views about it.

Whether the twentieth-century newspaper is to be big or little, tabloid or telefax, its intelligence, curiosity, and integrity will be no better than the education of the people who write it and read it. The mold of the common man's newspaper will be cast in the public schools. A thought that should give tremendous pause.

4. Radio, TV, and the Common Man

In the Thirty Years' War between the broadcasters and their critics, the heavy battalions and God—as represented by the public—have been on the broadcasters' side. If television hadn't revived some ancient misgivings and made some early blunders, serious criticism of the broadcasting industry might have disappeared entirely; the critics had become fretful and ineffective, and the broadcasters—who had been occasionally apologetic—were so secure in public favor that they showed few symptoms of the guilt complex that had haunted them in their earlier phases. As far as the public was concerned the critics were asking irrelevant questions, withholding praise where it was clearly due, and setting themselves up as the enemy of whatever was popular. The coming of television gives the critics a second chance to ask the right questions and thereby arrive at a useful relation to the industry.

The question being considered in this symposium is one of the right ones. And as it applies to broadcasting

45

it can be put in simple terms: Is it true, as has often been said, that the broadcasters underestimate the taste, intelligence, and maturity of the public? Are the masses ahead of the media?

Oversimplified like this, the question is also overloaded. The critics are asking the broadcasters, "How much longer do you intend to go on beating your wives?" and the broadcasters' answer is usually a combination of "We aren't legally married" and "They love it."

Obviously you can't discuss the relationship between broadcasters and audience until you know what an audience is. If you dig down to the bedrock on which the industry is founded, these solid facts become apparent: (1) an audience is what the sponsor buys; (2) an audience is what the broadcasters deliver; (3) an audience is a measurable fraction of the audience; (4) all the fractional audiences put together fall short of being "the public." Not at all apparent, but confirmed by experience, is the hypothesis that audiences are created by broadcasting.

The fundamental attitudes toward audiences are all simple. Broadcasters (including sponsors) attempt to satisfy the current wants of large sections of the total audience; critics assert that the people making up these audiences have other interests and curiosities, perhaps not intense enough to be called wants, but legitimate; they also assert that the definite wants of smaller, but sizable, audiences should also be satisfied. And the government, representing us as the third party in the discussion, licenses broadcasters to operate "in the public interest," which transcends all partial interests and is greater than their sum. It is, for instance, in the public interest that a vast number of citizens should be alert and intelligent enough to meet the successive crises of the world today, and it is therefore against the public interest if broadcasting fails to contribute to our awareness of problems and our capacity to solve them. But the individual broadcaster can be and usually is absolved of this responsibility.

The fact that an audience is a commodity to be bought and sold is usually concealed, because technically sponsors buy "time on the air." But both the jargon of the trade and some recent rulings of the FCC indicate that what is actually bought is the time and attention given by the audience. To attract sponsors, broadcasters often promise to build an audience for a chosen time-period, and there is ample evidence that audiences have been prevented from coming into existence. The hypothesis stated above can be expanded: audiences are created by broadcasts and exist only at those times and in those places that the broadcasters want them to exist.

This is the central fact about broadcasting, because it is the central fact about the audience, but its implications are so grave that I think some proof must be brought forward. There's a lot of it.

Several years ago CBS issued an effective promotion piece called "Our Sixty-ninth-Most-Popular-Program"; it pointed out that although sixty-eight other programs on the network had higher ratings, "Invitation to Learning" still had an impressive audience of over a million listeners. At about the same time (according to FCC records) "Invitation to Learning" was being heard on only thirty-nine CBS stations; ninety-seven other affiliates of the network did not carry the program. No proof exists that any significant number of people in these ninety-seven other cities demanded to hear "Invitation to Learning," but common sense rejects the idea that nobody in ninety-seven average cities wouldn't be glad to hear a program that a million people in thirty-nine other cities listened to with pleasure. That an audience in the ninety-seven cities did not come into being was simply because the creative act, making the program available, was not performed.

The same thing has happened on other networks and with all kinds of programs. Thus 216 Mutual stations did not carry a round-table discussion and only 40 did; a Labor for Victory program during the war was taken by 35 NBC stations, refused by 104; and so on. We do not yet have comparable data for television, but the principle is the same.

Parallel and opposite is the case of symphonic music. The precarious lives of great orchestras in pre-radio days, their constant "drives" for endowment funds, indicate that at most a few hundred thousand musical individuals actively wanted to hear the classics. This hardly constituted a demand by broadcasting standards. It is a matter of record that when William S. Paley proposed to broadcast the concerts of the New York Philharmonic-Symphony he knew that an audience for them did not exist and declared his intention of creating one. He was successful; eventually the Philharmonic even acquired a sponsor and its audience was at one time estimated at about ten million. The demand is so intense that an attempt to broadcast the concerts by transcription, at various hours, brought violent objections and was abandoned after a single season.

The effect of symphonic broadcasts and other musical programs on concert-going and the sale of classical records—some $50,000,000 a year spent on the first and 40 per cent of all record sales for the latter—are in a sense secondary proofs of the creative power of broadcasting. The primary effect is radio's own audience. In creating this audience sponsors were unable to afford the long pull; they paid for orchestral music but withdrew support after a short time, so that it required a network with all its resources (and the happy coincidence of unsold time on the air) to sustain the programs long enough to let the audience form, to let enough people know that they didn't dislike "long-hair" music as much as they thought they did. Again, considering broadcasting only, and not cultural effects, it should be noted that the significance of this entire episode lies not in the fact that the music was good and serious, but that the broadcasters offered all kinds of music, widening the area of choice; if the prevalent mode had been classical and the broadcasters had created an audience for hot music, the moral would still be the same: audiences are created by programs.

There is a more significant but less spectacular case in which the broadcasters acted in the public interest far ahead of public demand. They began to supply international news and commentary of a high order in the 1930's, at a time when the people at large preferred not to be troubled by such matters, a period of marked self-absorption in domestic affairs and strong isolationism. These programs were unsponsored for many years, and almost without exception they demanded real mental activity on the part of the listener to match the alert intelligence of the correspondents abroad. These broadcasts were a specific case of giving the public what the public ought to have—and no damned nonsense about what the public wants; and I believe that the high level of emotional stability of the American people after Pearl Harbor is largely due to the creation of an audience, of substantial size, aware of the international situation. This is one of the most honorable services radio has rendered to our country, and I think the industry ought to be proud of it, without reservation.

But the industry does make a reservation, in principle. It cannot accept the Paley principle of creative broadcasting because of the responsibility that principle implies. For you cannot logically say, "We created the audience for great music and for the discussion of public affairs, but in the case of neurotic daytime serials and sadistic murder playlets we weren't creative at all, we were merely satisfying a demand that already existed." Demand is generalized and diffuse—for entertainment, for thrills, for vicarious sadness, for laughs; it can be satisfied by programs of different types and different qualities; and only after these programs have been offered is there any demand for them. Supply comes first in this business and creates its own demand.

A few months ago *Time* published a letter from a reader in Nigeria which gives a perfect, though extreme, instance of this principle. The writer said: "In the Gold

Coast one movie owner possesses only two features, *King Kong* and *The Mark of Zorro*. . . . On Mondays, Tuesdays and Fridays he has packed them in for years with the former; [the other three weekdays he shows the latter] . . . . On Sunday there is always a surefire double feature—*King Kong* and *The Mark of Zorro*." I submit that this enterprising exhibitor began by satisfying an unspecific demand for entertainment, then created an audience for a specific kind of entertainment, and finally prevented an audience for any other kind of entertainment from coming into existence.

Our mass media, the movies as well as radio and television, offer a greater variety of entertainments, but they are for the most part aimed at the same intellectual level and call for the same emotional responses, the level and the responses being relatively low. The challenge to the mind comes infrequently, and we are being conditioned to make frequent emotional responses of low intensity— the quick nervous reaction to melodrama and the quick laugh at everything else. If material cannot be adapted to give the thrill or the laugh, it is thrown out. A spectacular instance of this occurred recently in the Ford anniversary show, where the entire story of life in the United States in the past half-century was reduced to vaudeville, the violent strikes of the 1920's being presented as part of a jocular newsreel, the Depression in a ballet, and the revolution of the New Deal, being intractable, omitted entirely. It was a very successful program, and its success is part of the conditioning process which I call creative, by which the audience is persuaded that it is getting all it can ever want.

Statistical evidence exists that actually the audience —the public, to be more accurate—wants more. I place few bets on the automatic answer given to researchers, "Yes, we would like more serious programs on the air," because, for one thing, some of the respondents call quiz shows educational and because this "want" is a pious aspiration as diffused and uncertain as what the broadcasters say they get from the public. Yet it is noteworthy that all the researchers point in the same direction: people at every level of education, in significant numbers, do imply some dissatisfaction with the programs they are getting, and among these there are ten million people, not habitual book readers, not college graduates, who consistently ask for programs of a higher intellectual content. (Book readers and college graduates make the same request twice as often, but they are numerically less important. All these figures come from studies made for the industry.)

Direct corroborative evidence comes from the report of the FM stations; the Lowell Institute station in Boston, wholly educational, has a constantly increasing audience of unswerving loyalty; and the University of Michigan, broadcasting at unfavorable hours, within a small area, has an audience for its TV programs large enough to indicate that the same programs transmitted at good hours over a national network would attract a sponsorable audience.

The evidence favorable to the broadcasters (in music, for instance) and the unfavorable evidence (the prevalence of third-rate crime programs, let us say) come together at this point. If the broadcasters accept their social responsibility, they can continue to pile up huge profits without corrupting the taste and undermining the mental activity of the audience. Sponsors, agencies, packagers, stations, and networks taken together have created the kinds of wants they could satisfy, and while broadcasting has not lost audiences—as the movies have —by repeating the sure thing over and over again, there have always been vast untouched segments of the public. (At the time the two major networks were offering daytime serials all day long and protesting that women wouldn't listen to anything else, 76 per cent of all women who had radios in such a city as Boston were simply not listening; within a few years it was discovered that women would listen to many other kinds of programs.) It takes time, intelligence, and conviction to face the simple mathematical fact that one is not the only common denominator of four and eight and sixteen and sixty-four. The broadcasters have ratings which prove to their satisfaction that a sufficient number of separate individuals watch each of the one hundred or more programs of violence on television every week, but that is no proof of public demand for so many of these programs and it certainly is not proof that other kinds of programs would not build up equally satisfactory audiences.

The huge costs of television production have introduced a new element. The pure sustaining program of radio, experimental and not intended for sale, has disappeared, and the status of television may now be described as "commercialism mitigated by Foundations." "American Inventory" (Sloan) and "Omnibus" (Ford) are essentially comparable to network sustaining programs in radio, and all the networks and many stations are bringing in inexpensive programs from museums and universities with or without special endowments or other funds for broadcasting. Broadcasters have been glad to shift the burden of costs for such programs. Provided a sufficient number of them continue on the air, it doesn't matter to the public who pays the bill.

Other developments also point to the same ill-defined feeling that commercial broadcasting alone cannot satisfy all the legitimate wants of the public. Grand opera has been "narrowcast" into theatres, the audience paying admission, and there are a dozen plans to handle plays in a similar way. And while pay-as-you-go transmission of movies is more an economic move than a social one, it adds another variant from the standard commercial system. "Omnibus," the most successful of the experiments, makes the point of divergence particularly clear. It seems to assume that the usual commercial sponsor is not bound by any social duty to take long risks, to keep a program running until its audience forms; the program is therefore produced (as all radio programs were in the beginning) without reference to or interference from the sponsor, but is made available for sponsorship on these terms. Doing what neither the network nor the sponsor can do, such a program signifies that an area outside their capacities must be cultivated if television is to be satisfactory, not only to particular audiences, but to the public as a whole.

We know, in sum, that the broadcasting business has been ahead of the public as well as behind it. We know that better programs often fail to get support. One reason for this is that the better programs are often conceived as something totally different from good programs—the rhetorical documentaries of Norman Corwin, for instance—and not, as they should be, as a constant improvement in the quality of programs already proved acceptable. Another reason is that the volume and velocity of the average program surfeits the appetite and makes it progressively less likely that a keener taste will develop.

It is at this point that the broadcasters share responsibility with other manipulators of the public. They dodge it by the ancient excuse of giving the public what it wants, conceiving the public as a mass with tastes already formed. Once they admit that the media can raise or lower the public taste, in the very act of satisfying the public demand, they will come closer to their function, which is defined legally as operating in the public interest, and which, morally, does not insist on raising the public taste but demands, as a minimum, that the public be given every opportunity to find its own level of taste by having access to the best as well as to the mean— which, in this case, is far from golden.

5. Hollywood Verdict: Gilt but Not Guilty

I HAVE a profound respect for experts—in all fields except my own. When they assure us that there has been a substantial advance in the past decade in American appreciation of literature, drama, and music I unhesitatingly accept their happy findings. But when they assert, as they frequently do, that similar progress has taken place in movie taste I can only caution hold your horses—or at least your 3–D glasses.

There is considerable justification for the indictment so frequently presented against the movie moguls that they themselves have, over the years, fashioned their own audience and are now saddled with it—an audience avid for escape, acquiescent to saccharine formulae, and allergic to what it disparagingly terms "message" pictures. On the other hand, I am unfortunately so venerable that I vividly recall the resentment of picturegoers when Goldwyn released *The Cabinet of Dr. Caligari*, the first full-length film to challenge the reign of realism on the screen; I remember, too, the catastrophic failure of Von Stroheim's *Greed,* probably the most cinematically imaginative American picture ever made, and the other similar mishaps too numerous to catalogue which overtook adventurous pioneers who in early movie days overestimated the intelligence of their public. Little, however, can be gained by seeking to establish the relative guilt of producers, exhibitors, and the public. They all share in the errors of the past and the perplexities of the present.

At least I am perplexed, although not my highbrow friends. Almost daily for the past thirty years they have assured me that the public is at last eager for more adult, thought-provoking pictures than it is receiving. Whether they have arrived at this cheerful conclusion through research, revelation, or merely wishful thinking I am not aware. It seems to me, after a lifetime largely devoted to the pursuit of patrons, that there are many publics, and that nobody knows with any degree of consistency what any of these publics wants—neither Spyros Skouras, the indefatigable president of Twentieth Century-Fox, nor his critics, nor the various publics themselves. Of the three, however, I distrust Mr. Skouras's judgments the least. He, at any rate, makes his guesses neither on the basis of hunch nor hope but on a continuing study of his company's finances and their fluctuations with its films—good, bad, and indifferent. Indeed, if we really desire to be helpful rather than hep it would be well to stop indulging in the time-honored sport of throwing spite-balls at Mr. Skouras and his fellow movie magnates—if for no other reason than that they have become experts at dodging them. Moreover, as the captain of the *Texas* shouted to his sailors when the Spanish ships off Santiago were sinking, "Don't cheer, those poor devils are dying." If we are genuinely interested in the production of more "mature films" (to use a phrase that I detest but do not know how to improve) let's stop talking loosely about how the producers underestimate their public and analyze what have been the roadblocks encountered by such films and to what extent they can, under existing conditions, be destroyed or bypassed.

Briefly, they can be summarized as follows:

(1) The fabulous financial success of the industry discouraged experimentation and the search for marginal markets.

(2) The equally fabulous cost of Hollywood picture-producing made mass appeal the safest and quickest method of assuring a profit.

(3) Most of the so-called "prestige" movies which were produced, and the foreign films which were imported, failed to receive sufficient public support to encourage increased activities of this nature.

At the outset we must disabuse our minds of the stereotype of the illiterate movie tycoon with the twelve-year-old mentality. Anyone who regards Mr. Schenck of M-G-M or Mr. Balaban of Paramount as lacking horse sense had better not try horse trading with them. Neither of these unassuming, likable gentlemen went to college, but if they had they surely would have made Phi Beta Kappa and been elected "the man most apt to succeed" in their respective classes.

They and their competitors have only seen fit to submit to the iron laws of capitalist economics rather than to the equally inflexible precepts of contemporary uplifters. If, as they found out early in their careers, wonderful pictures like Bob Flaherty's starve and Shirley Temple films break attendance records, it appeared prudent to them to pay more deference to little girls with dimples than to distinguished explorers with a yen for showing how strange people live and think in distant places. If controversial films provided little cash and many repercussions from pressure groups of every hue, company presidents anxious to retain their jobs and emoluments decreed fewer dramatic treatments of the burning issues of the day like *The Watch on the Rhine* and more excursions into never-never land like *Lost Horizon.* If Robert Montgomery fans were shocked when he appeared in *Night Must Fall* as a psychopathic murderer rather than in his customary role of a light and debonair lover, studio executives concluded that typecasting was what their public preferred and thenceforward heroes remained heroic and bad men persisted in their villainies.

There were annual gestures, indeed more than are generally acknowledged, in the direction of biography, art, and defiance of formula, such as *Abe Lincoln in Illinois, The Long Way Home,* and *The Ox-Bow Incident,* but they met with so little popular favor that prudent presidents followed the line of least resistance, and —like the manufacturers of automobiles or zippers—gave the customers what they seemed most eager to pay for. They regarded their obligation to their stockholders as more pressing than the educational and cultural needs of the nation. While we must deplore this strictly com-

59

mercial approach to the operation of a great medium of communication, we must also remember that had they acted otherwise they would quickly have been replaced by hungry rivals more rapacious and even less civic-minded.

Conducting the industry as a business rather than as a social trust, they created a world-wide entertainment empire the like of which had never been conceived before. The courts have judged them guilty of conspiracy in the distribution and exhibition of their wares, but in production cut-throat competition prevailed. The battle for stars, stories, and technicians beggars description and would have beggared any less indestructible an enterprise. Production budgets zoomed to astronomic heights. Efficiency experts representing banks and other gimlet-eyed investors journeyed regularly to Hollywood to see who was crazy and returned home raving maniacs themselves. As costs continued to soar, so inevitably did the pressure for a mass market. During the thirties and forties this was maintained by trade practices such as producer-ownership of the leading theater circuits and the block-booking system under which exhibitors seeking to purchase major box-office attractions were also compelled to buy the less desirable pictures. When the courts eventually declared these procedures illegal, and every picture had to be sold strictly on its merits, or what passed for merits, it had to be fashioned and merchandised even more than previously for its appeal to the widest (frequently interpreted as synonymous with the lowest) common denominator of public taste. Under the much-abused system of block-booking, unpretentious

films with novel situations and fresh attitudes, such as
A Man to Remember or *The Curse of the Cat People,*
occasionally crept through and were crammed down the
throats of helpless exhibitors. Now, in the classic words
of *Variety,* it was "boffo or busto," meaning there was
no longer any middle ground and every picture was
either a click or a cluck.

Most commentators fret about the ethics of the industry, but what actually went hopelessly haywire was
its economics. The average negative cost at Twentieth
Century-Fox in 1949 was $2,200,000 and other major
studios did not lag far behind. Orson Welles recently re-
marked: "If I am a painter and want to paint I go out,
buy an easel, some paints and brushes, and go to work.
I am an artist. But if I want to make a moving picture I
have to raise a million dollars. And when I do that I become a businessman."

A modest theatrical production can be staged for
forty thousand dollars; a novel with a sale of some eight
thousand copies can pay its way; CBS regards a listening audience of a million as "impressive." But the average Hollywood feature film to return its investment must
be seen by at least fifteen million people. In the face of
the need for so vast an audience only an occasional dar-
ing producer, such as John Huston or Stanley Kramer,
tempts fate with a *Red Badge of Courage* or a *Member
of the Wedding.* Such pictures frequently are referred
to as "artistic failures" although they may play to audiences of five to ten million which, by any other standard than Hollywood's inflated production costs, would
be ample to return a huge profit. Under its present set-

up the industry can and does turn out fine entertaining pictures which appeal to every class in the community such as *From Here to Eternity* or *Roman Holiday*, but those who seek subtlety or sophistication will not find it in their movies any more frequently than they do so in the pages of the *Ladies Home Journal* or *Cosmopolitan*.

Because of this or in spite of it, or probably because all other desirable commodities were rationed while cash was plentiful, the public flocked to the movies in the years following World War II as never before. The profits of the six leading companies in 1946 amounted to $332,-000,000. Weekly domestic theater attendance was estimated, probably somewhat generously, at 80,000,000.

And then almost overnight television reared its ugly antennae on the rooftops of the nation. Within four years twenty-five million living rooms were converted into miniature theaters. Movie men, softened by years of easy success, faced a youthful aggressive competitor which was prepared, through commercial sponsorship, to furnish entertainment gratis—maybe not so lavish or star-studded as Hollywood's, but entertainment minus queues, minus parking, minus baby-sitters, minus box office.

Producers and exhibitors alike reeled under the impact. Receipts declined 44 per cent and over 5,000 of the 18,500 conventional indoor type of theaters closed. To combat the challenge of television M-G-M and Twentieth Century-Fox, at that time the best organized and most alert studios in Hollywood (though maybe I think so only because they diagnosed the malady much as I did), decided that the time was ripe to supply the screens of the nation with a product directed at a higher intellectual level than had in the past proved palatable or profitable. The addicts of quantity in entertainment could, they figured, linger at home, hugging their consoles as well as their consorts, while those who preferred quality would at long last find their more rarefied tastes gratified with greater frequency at their local theater.

Never before had these two companies, thanks to their gifted studio heads, Dore Schary and Darryl Zanuck, so copiously expended their resources and talents to create a superior product. Never before had they turned out so high a percentage of adult films. And never before did they suffer such catastrophic consequences. Movies were better than ever, but business was worse. *Intruder in the Dust, Asphalt Jungle, Magnificent Yankee, Fourteen Hours, S. S. Teakettle, Decision Before Dawn,* one after another proved resounding flops. If they had not released a few massive spectacles like *Quo Vadis* and *David and Bathsheba* and a few smash musicals like *The Great Caruso* and *Showboat,* and if their foreign markets had not greatly expanded, both companies would have shown heavy losses. As it was, Twentieth's earnings at the height of its liaison with the adult, if not the adulterous, nose-dived to one cent per share.

Confronted by disaster, they rapidly reversed their field. The sensational success of Cinerama and of the first 3–D quickie, *Bwana Devil,* suggested a new and more promising method of enticing patrons back to the picture palaces. Overnight the industry was again looking at the future through rose-colored glasses, if only by courtesy of the Polaroid Company of America. What price maturity if Warner's *House of Wax* or Paramount's *Sangaree* could bring out crowds the like of which had not been seen since 1947? Mr. Harry Warner was so enthralled that he prophesied that a pair of polarizing glasses would soon become as essential to the average man's wardrobe as a wristwatch or a fountain pen. Mr. Milton Gunzberg, proponent of something called "natural vision," declared that those who attended it "received as much eye benefit in some instances as they might from experiencing a dozen treatments for exercises in a doctor's office."

Suddenly we all became authorities on interaxial spacing, distorted convergence, and anamorphic lenses. Never since the advent of sound had there been so much excitement in Hollywood, and never—even then—so much confusion. Almost every day the trade papers heralded the invention of some new scheme for showing stereoscopic or wide-screen pictures or both. There was Depth-O-Vision, Metrovision, and Paravision, Vistorama, Triorama, TriOpticon, True Stereo, and Bolex Stereo. The Russians, as was to be anticipated, announced that they had scooped the universe and had been showing 3–D films without glasses for lo these many years.

This is neither the suitable place, nor am I the suitable authority, to adequately explain these technical innovations. Suffice it to say that the indomitable Mr. Skouras emerged with perhaps the best and certainly the most publicized process. Christened CinemaScope, it dispenses with the glasses required for 3–D and the three projectors which make Cinerama too costly for widespread theater installation. It is projected on a huge curved screen, with a width more than two and one-half times its height, and accompanied by a cacophonic roar known as stereophonic sound. Actually, the picture projected is not stereoscopic, but is designed to engulf and overwhelm theater patrons to such an extent that they feel themselves part and parcel of what they are witnessing. At least on the initial week of its showing at the Roxy Theater, *The Robe*, Twentieth Century-Fox's first CinemaScope masterpiece, overpowered the New York public to the tune of $317,000 (including taxes), establishing an all-time theatrical box-office record.

Mr. Skouras has announced that hereafter all of his company's productions will be shot exclusively for CinemaScope, and although exhibitors may bewail the cost of new equipment and esthetes its "mail slot" proportions, there can be little question that CinemaScope or some similar process has come to stay. Shortly after *The Robe* and *Quo Vadis* proved so successful, 124 films designed either for 3–D or the wide screen were put into production by different companies. The new processes call for "big pictures"—for the spectacular and the epic, rather than for the intimate and the tender. While these techniques are in the ascendancy, *Quo Vadis* will be the prevalent movie model rather than *Lili*.

The expense of producing such pictures makes all previous records appear miserly. Twentieth Century-Fox appropriated $35,000,000 for its first fourteen CinemaScope productions. Production schedules indicate that in the future the major companies will be producing less than half the number of pictures which Hollywood in its heyday used to produce each year, but the total outlay will probably be the greatest in its history.

The prospects for the future, however, are not as bleak and forbidding as all this may sound. There are many theaters which because of their limited size, bankroll, or enthusiasm, are unprepared to install 3–D and/or wide-angle lenses. There are many picturegoers who will find themselves unable to adjust to the eye and ear strain of the stereoscopic and stereophonic and who will declare themselves allergic to colossal closeups, lengthy scenes, and diminished tempo.

These recalcitrant exhibitors and patrons constitute potential recruits for what are now unfortunately known as "art houses." Actually, their name is no more misleading than are the reports, sedulously circulated by wishful thinkers, concerning their rapidly expanding numbers and prosperity. They rarely, except as an added attraction, play genuine art films such as *The Titan* or *Leonardo Da Vinci*—their current plight, if they did, would be even worse. Only those who occasionally manage to book such Hollywood forays into the adult world as *The Moon Is Blue* or *Death of a Salesman* show a reasonable return, if any, on their investment.

At present less than five hundred theaters play foreign and English films with reasonable consistency, and the majority of these do so only when a suitable product is available—said product being more apt to consist of *Bitter Rice* or *Anna,* with sex appeal thinly disguised as art, than of Continental films of genuine distinction such as *The Little World of Don Camillo* or *Forbidden Games*. One hundred twenty of them are located in the

New York metropolitan area, forty-four in Los Angeles, and thirty-four in San Francisco. In all, they exist in only seventy communities and they represent less than 3 per cent of the total number of theater seats in America.

The existence of this handful of houses is, however, of far greater consequence than their limited number or success would indicate. Its real significance is suggested by Frederick Lewis Allen in *The Big Change,* when he writes in quite another connection: "The job before those Americans who would like to see the United States a Greece rather than a Carthage is to try to develop, alongside the media of entertainment and equipment which satisfy the people's present needs, others which will satisfy more exacting taste and will be on hand for them when they are ready for more rewarding fare." Those of us who, like Mr. Allen, realize the necessity for such outposts of culture would be of greater service to our cause if we talked less glowingly about the progress of the art houses and sought more zealously to understand the nature of their current status.

Their problems are many. The two primary difficulties, however, consist of a scarcity of pictures and of patrons. The Sutton or the Paris Theaters in New York can flourish with three or four successful pictures a year, the Squirrel Hill in Pittsburgh may need twenty, but before the Roxy of Fargo, North Dakota, for example, can feel reasonably safe in abandoning a strictly commercial policy it requires the assurance of a steady flow of product. And until we have art theaters in the Fargos as well as in New York and Pittsburgh the movement will never be built on a solid national foundation.

Nor can it have such a solid foundation without ardent local supporters. The reactions of the nonhabitual moviegoers are, at best, tardy. It does not make a vital difference to a publisher if his book sells in the first week of its publication or in the tenth, but with movies prompt patronage is of the essence. Every first-run theater has a weekly holdover figure. If a picture falls below this amount of business it is losing money and few exhibitors have the intestinal fortitude to prolong the engagement in the hope that patronage will "build." After an unsuccessful showing of this nature it becomes almost impossible to obtain subsequent runs for a picture. The finest French film of the Resistance, *Bataille Du Rail,* for example, has been exhibited on less than half-a-dozen occasions. Time after time friends have told me that they heard that a picture which I was handling was superb and that they fully intended to see it. Before they could tear themselves away, however, from such agreeable pastimes as discussing how juvenile were most movies, it had been relegated to a can on a shelf, only occasionally dusted off for a select institutional showing.

The success of a limited number of English importations like *Tight Little Island, Kind Hearts and Coronets,* and *The Cruel Sea* at New York City small first-run houses has led to premature rejoicing among myopic Manhattanites. West of the Hudson, however, and south of the Bay, such films are still regarded with profound suspicion. Small-town patrons find their Oxford intonation so unintelligible that they suggest the need of subtitles similar to those used for French or Italian importations.

A few years ago my associates and I imported an English melodrama, *Seven Days to Noon,* which dealt in the atomic bomb. The picture grossed less than $225,-000 and of this disappointing figure we took about 65 per cent out of the New York metropolitan area. The average for a Hollywood picture for that territory is 15 per cent! *Hamlet* and *Henry V,* aided by the vigorous support of Women's Clubs, school authorities, and other public-spirited groups, which apparently Shakespeare can enlist but which we have never been able to muster for authors who have the misfortune to be alive, both grossed over two and one-half million dollars. But for every *Henry V* there are a dozen other English pictures which fail even to return the cost of prints, accessories, and advertising. Such splendid features as *Cry the Beloved Country, Ivory Hunter,* and *The Brave Don't Cry* will not transfer an American dime to their dollar-hungry creators. As for foreign-language films, their business, contrary to the general impression, has been steadily shrinking since the halcyon days of *Open City* and *Paisan.* Rarely do they succeed in obtaining two hundred bookings; fifty is much closer to the average, and many secure even less.

If the art theater is to justify its existence it must free itself from its present bondage to the films of foreign nations. Much as we may appreciate European realism and candor, it does not appear to me unduly jingoistic to believe that we also require pictures about the American scene written by American authors, directed by men with an American point of view, and performed by American actors. Fortunately, or unfortunately, there are many such men and women now available. Some of them are Hollywood exiles whose youthful idealism misled them into joining organizations which a decade or more ago gave the impression of being wholly praiseworthy in their objectives. Many of them in the past participated in making some of our best pictures. They are now out of work and eager to demonstrate their devotion to democratic rather than totalitarian ideals. In addition, there are the old-time non-idealogical rebels who never were able to adjust themselves to big studio practices or politics, not to mention the present brand of irreconcilables bitterly averse to the new epic techniques. Lastly, there is a talented younger generation knocking on the door—a door which with a production cut of probably 50 per cent will prove harder to pry open than ever before.

In the past, independent pictures—except for the costly creations of such intrepid entrepreneurs as Goldwyn and Selznick—have been almost exclusively imitative in intent. The films distributed by Lippert or Monogram were designed solely to duplicate with inferior casts, stories, and production facilities the successes of their bigger rivals. They were never intended for arthouse showing but only to serve as secondary attractions on double-feature bills.

There have, however, been a handful of exceptions, enough to prove that it is only by sufferance that Europe continues to enjoy its present monopoly in the field of the experimental or the sophisticated cinema—exceptions such as *The Quiet One, Navajo Boy, The Well* and *The Little Fugitive*. Bucking the present tendency towards the lush and the lavish, there are, even in Hollywood, young men like Clarence Greene, Russell Rouse, and others who apparently have mastered the art of making for $150,000 films that are not an insult to the intelligence.

Under existing conditions, however, pictures budgeted even at this low figure are unable to return a profit if exhibited exclusively in art houses. To cure this situation there should be at least 50 per cent more such theaters. They cannot continue to be confined to a limited number of highly competitive situations but must be spread across the country until there is one in each of the 106 American cities with populations of over 100,000, and at least two or three in the larger communities. What with bad business, shortages of product, and the dilemma of the new techniques, there are a plethora of commercial theaters prepared to experiment with a new policy. They will do so just as soon as suitable pictures in adequate quantities are available. And such pictures will, in turn, be available just as soon as more patrons rally to the support of those now in circulation.

Neither of the ancient bogeys—Hollywood moguls or inflexible exhibitors—stand in the way. All that is necessary is for the intellectuals to stop paying lip service to the better cinema and to start paying admission. When they do so the exciting thing about American movies will be, not how much wider they are, but how much better.

6. The Garret and the Masterpiece

T HE creative artist needs help. He has always needed help. But it is curious that, in an age which has produced the necessary wealth to support creative effort, and the mass media to give them currency and recognition, the artist is achieving neither the help he deserves nor the vehicles necessary to his own fulfillment. Some of the reasons for this state of affairs grow out of three misconceptions concerning the creative arts in general and creative people in particular.

The first of these misconceptions is the one which says that the artist or writer or musician or independent scholar does not have to be supported because, if he has something in him that deserves to find expression, it will come out anyway. Related to this is the misconception that creative people work best under conditions of personal stress.

Over the years we have been in a position to observe the ways in which authors and artists work. We know of dozens of cases in which demonstrated creative ability

72

has been dammed up waiting the proper conditions for release, but where the conditions never materialized. We know of young authors whose first books were lavishly praised but who never had the chance to develop or test their talent. We know of young artists whose early work won prizes in exhibitions but whose spirit was broken because they could not eat blue ribbons or cash favorable reviews. Many of these artists turned commercial "just to keep going." A few of them were able after several years to resume their careers as serious painters. Most of them, however, had their feelings of romance for painting so dimmed as the result of day-in-and-out pressures that they never did make the journey back. Nor can they be universally blamed. A society which venerates material success as a social and frequently as a moral yardstick cannot in good conscience blame the artist for mirroring those values.

In any event, we must scotch the fallacy that good artists, writers, musicians, or scholars are not affected by personal adversity. For every story of a famous artist who continued to work creatively despite hunger, sickness, and misery, there are countless instances of those who stopped working when they stopped eating. Cervantes might have done more if he hadn't been demoralized by hardship. Vondel, frequently referred to as the Dutch Shakespeare, carried on as long as he could despite intense privation, then gave up. Camoens, the Portuguese poet, receiving a complaint that he had failed to deliver verses as promised, replied: "When I wrote verses while a young man, I had sufficient food, was a lover, and beloved by many friends and by the ladies.

Then I felt poetical ardor. Now I have no spirits, no peace of mind." Camoens's former servant tried to keep him alive by going out on the streets at night foraging and begging for food.

Balzac made money and had no trouble spending it. Whatever his personal inadequacy as a budget-balancer, however, we do know that he worked poorly or not at all when unable to pay his bills. Rossini was accused of prostituting his vast talent for money. He made little effort to refute the charge; it takes money to live. Christopher Smart, like any number of his contemporaries, enjoyed the benefactions of a patron. When the patron died, Smart's pension dried up and none other was forthcoming. Like ordinary mortals, he cracked up under adverse circumstances, was confined to an asylum, and died at the age of forty-nine.

The poverty of Pierre Corneille has frequently been exaggerated. What is true, however, is that the eminent dramatist-poet occasionally suspended his work because he was in debt. It is said that Racine once found him in a state of acute hunger, reported the fact to Louis XIV, who only then sent Corneille enough money to get going again. Isaac Disraeli, who is authority for the story, also quotes from a petition to Parliament by the Marquis of Worcester during the reign of Charles II, asking for money to finance himself and to publish his "Centenary of Inventions." The money was not granted and the account of the inventions was lost. There is reason to believe, says Disraeli, that inventions similar to the steam-engine and telegraph were among them.

Perhaps only one other poet in English literature can

match Spenser's gift for perfectionism in verse. Yet Spenser died, in Ben Jonson's words, "for lack of bread." True, he died under circumstances of political strife so great that the actual cause of his death may have been obscured. But there can be no doubt that his later years were robbed of productiveness because of poverty. As he himself wrote:

> *Full little knowest thou, that*
> > *hast not try'd,*
> *What Hell it is, in suing long*
> > *to bide.*

and:

> *To fawn, to crouch, to wait,*
> > *to ride, to run,*
> *To speed, to give, to want, to*
> > *be undone.*

What emerges from all this is not the determination of the artist to create despite all obstacles but the fact that the artist has frequently been hurt or diminished because of the bland assumption that an artist is a somewhat separate species capable of living indefinitely on art and adulation.

The second general misconception is that literature or music or art, if only it is good enough, will pay its own way through public acceptance.

The contemporary refutation of this fallacy is Gian-Carlo Menotti. He is now generally regarded as one of the most gifted young writers of serious music in America; yet his work, however excellent, has for the most part failed to pay its own way. *The Medium* and *The Telephone* did not pay their own way when first produced. It was only the intervention of a few sponsors who believed in Menotti that kept the operas going.

Hundreds of American writers, painters, and musicians have benefited from the grants of foundations, the most active of which in this particular field has been the Guggenheim. Out of all these grants has come an impressive number of artistic creations which do considerable credit to both artist and foundation. There is scarcely a first-rate publisher whose lists have not been enhanced through such works, many of which the publisher himself could not have afforded to underwrite. If we make the statement that these books would somehow have been written or published even without foundation support, we may be only partially right. And to the extent that we may be partially wrong, we would have been deprived of books and paintings and music and scholarship which I think on analysis we would have regarded as serious losses.

In the old days, an artist had a patron or friends or took pains with his dedications. Dedicatees, at least in those days, could usually be counted upon to kick in with some negotiable appreciation. Galland, translator of the *Arabian Nights,* was thoughtful enough to dedicate each tale to a different person. No one knows what the average dedication brought, but at least Galland was sufficiently enterprising to pick the one literary property with more tales than most books have pages. One thousand and one may not be an even number but it probably was converted into a nice round sum.

Galland wasn't the only creative person who knew the advantage of omnibus dedications. When Chapman translated Homer, sixteen of the sonnets were dedicated to various lords and ladies. And Spenser found it necessary to include no fewer than fifteen special-address sonnets in *The Faerie Queene* to actual and potential benefactors. Dryden's dedications were so thick and syrupy that it seems scarcely possible that they weren't even more embarrassing to the patrons than to the author himself. Maybe that was the way it was intended to be. The ego can travel a long way before it knows it has been taken for a ride, but surely it must want to get out and walk home when comparisons are made to Divinity.

All of the foregoing is intended to suggest three things. First, that it is not necessarily true that the creative person can create with or without vitamins. Second, that not every work of art has been supported on its merits, if, indeed, it has been supported at all. Third, that certain forms of support for the artist are degrading, demoralizing, and debilitating. They harm not only the artist but the community-at-large. A good artist is a prism for refracting beauty and truth; he is to be supported not because it is thoughtful to keep people from being hungry—that is the function of charity or government—but because the human community cannot live fully or joyously unless its sense of beauty is exercised and proclaimed. It is the artist's job to deal with these things of beauty in order to provide not necessarily a joy forever but a touch of loveliness that will last as long as society's capacity for beauty will last.

This brings us to the next misconception detrimental

to the humanities: That great art is something which by its very nature endures, is never lost, and therefore does not have to be specially supported or protected when it is first brought into being, assuming one is able to recognize it for the work of genius that it is.

We begin with the first part of this fallacy. We pay both honor and attention to the Greeks and the Romans, as we should, but we have so far mined only a fraction of the cultural treasures of those times. This is not to say that Plato, Aristotle, Thucydides *et al* were a mere sampling of an Athenian constellation as yet far beyond our historical range finders. What it does mean is that cosmic classical riches have been lost not only through carelessness but through ignorance. Juvenal, Persius, and Martial have fared well, but can we say the same of Livy or Cicero or Virgil or Horace or Sophocles or Aeschylus or Xenophon or Aristophanes? It was only the sheerest accident which made it possible for Cicero's *De Republica* to come to light. This key item of Cicero's essays had served as the base for a surprinting of a tract on the psalms and was not discovered until 1823. Another valuable Cicero essay, *De Gloria,* spoken of so glowingly by Petrarch, may never come to light; its last known address was a nineteenth-century pawn shop. Let us not forget that Quintilian was discovered in a rubbish heap in a monastery of St. Gallo; that the original manuscript of Justinian's Pandects was discovered in Calabria by the Pisans; that the works of Agopard were about to be used to reinforce bindings in a book-binder's shop in Lyon when they were accidentally discovered by Papirius Masson; and that one of the original Magna

Chartas, with all its fancy seals and signatures, was discovered by Sir Robert Cotton, in one hand of a tailor, poised scissors in the other hand ready to cut into the parchment to make measuring slips. Still other instances: The manuscript of Montaigne's *Journal of his Travels to Italy* was not published until many generations after it had been written, when it was finally uncovered in a worm-eaten coffer in Montaigne's former chateau. Lady Mary Wortley Montagu's Letters were lost by her lawyer in his own office. Some non-legal reason no doubt. The propensity of lawyers, publishers, and editors for this sort of thing is a historic fact, as bewildered authors and their estates can attest. But one might as soon attempt to reform the solar system as set about reforming the desk habits of editors and lawyers.

The most famous discovery, of course, is a contemporary one. The literary imagination prides itself on its shockproof faculty, but it was staggered a few years ago when announcement was made of the appearance of the Boswell papers. Few stories in literature can compare with the towering drama of such treasures so long hidden and then suddenly coming to light.

And what of the countless hundreds of other manuscripts and early editions that have rotted in attics or trunks, or that were dumped or burned and whose very existence at one time was not even a matter of record? What about the books that died as manuscripts not because of lack of intrinsic worth but because a publisher may not have had the resources or the judgment or the imagination or the confidence to accept them? What about physical difficulties in the way of publishing books and keeping them alive?

79

Most importantly, what about the destruction of books or works of art for destruction's sake? Clarence Day to the contrary, a good book can die—through murder and, more especially, through neglect. So far as book burnings are concerned, where manuscripts or other copies are available, the books survive. But when the destroyer is able to burn the only existing copies, the books die. So far as neglect is concerned, consider Alexandria. At one time, Alexandria was the greatest literary and artistic city in the world. Whether with respect to its library, its art treasures, or the creative activities of its citizens, Alexandria was a forcing-house of genius. It could have been another Athens. But it wasn't. Over a period of time, the conditions of creative activity were altered or damaged. Wars, sickness, human depletion, crassness combined to destroy Alexandria. The famous library didn't die all at once. For a long period before Caliph Omar arrived on his leveling expedition the library was slowly dying of neglect—always more destructive than combustion. Incidentally, the most valuable item lost or destroyed in the Alexandrian library was the master list or catalogue file. Hundreds of thousands of manuscripts were lost; and there is no record to tell us what these manuscripts were or the subject matter they covered.

Yes, books can die of burning or neglect. And no one knows how many books which had been conceived in the minds of their authors were never written. Hitler did more than merely burn books; he burned the creators of books. There is no answer to this system of preventive cultural assassination. No answer, that is, except one. That is the inspired resolution of free men to keep alive the conditions of creative progress against all attackers—from within no less than from without.

When Hitler himself died in the great fire of Berlin, the ultimate challenge to human decency and progress did not die with him. Today, in many parts of the world, art and culture are being poured into stultifying political molds. And artistic and cultural sterilization has been practiced on numberless men of genius. No one knows what magnificent compositions within the original creative potential of Shostakovich will never be produced because in that society the worst thing that can happen to a man is, not to create bad art or music, but to be a deviationist. And to dozens of Shostakovich's colleagues, whether in music or art or literature, the gift of a creative potential will be meaningless so long as their work will be reviewed not by free critics but by the state itself. No state in history has known enough to do a successful job of cultural criticism. Government is difficult enough without having to take upon itself and unto itself the job of defining the good, the true, and the beautiful.

I stress this last point because the question of how best to contribute to the humanities—inside or outside the university—must not be confined to a narrow answer. Even before we contribute money, we must contribute convictions. We can put those convictions to work today in protecting a free and creative society. We can contribute our services to the fight against conformity. Contributing our decibels to the vocal fight against totalitarian suppression abroad is not enough. There is the need to contribute our voices and our energies to a mobilization at home against know-nothingism and cultural vigilantism. We can contribute the products of good sense in not allowing a free society to be destroyed by home-grown and self-appointed dictators of the public morality who expect that they have only to utter the words "anti-Communist" to qualify as leaders. The fight against communism will not be won by reducing our liberties but by enlarging them; not by imitating the Communist in his police-state psychology but by respecting and indeed exalting the strength of an open society; not by peddling slogans but by a careful understanding of what it is we are resisting and what it is we intend to keep.

It is not necessarily true that the artist or writer is an aloof figure who is disdainful of the surrounding community. When the community itself has respect for the artist, when it develops a sense of responsibility towards the creative life, we will find that the artist will need no further inducement to become an actively proud and proudly active member of that community.

7. Business and the State of Our Culture

ANY examination of the state of culture in America and any attempt to speculate about its prospects should take into full account the importance of big business as an all-pervading influence in our contemporary civilization. There is nothing new, to be sure, in recognizing the growth of business, of industry, and of the intricate network of interests related to them as dominant factors on which the material welfare of our society depends. It seems less widely recognized that our cultural welfare, our entertainment, our communication, and our arts are now for the most part also in the hands of large commercial enterprises and are therefore subject to many of the same pressures which shape other business operations. "What's good for General Motors" may be good for the country economically, but it hardly follows that what best sells Chevrolets best serves our cultural interests.

The trend to great size in the companies that furnish us with goods and services has paralleled the growth of the nation. The advantages of big business and its dangers have been the subject of continuing discussion. Aside from fears of monopolistic control, there have been many to regret that in so many fields the small independent operator, long a symbol of private enterprise, has had to give way to great corporations, as the corner grocer has had to bow to the chain stores and the supermarkets whose efficient management and huge purchasing power bring larger value and more variety to the customer. Something always considered attractive by society also disappears when individually produced work, particularly in skilled crafts, is priced out of the markets by the ever more remarkable output of machines.

The tangible benefits of large scale operations are all around us and are easy to see. Such losses as we may have suffered are less obvious, and when we try to assess cultural levels, we are primarily considering intangibles. Since the dramatic expansion in the accessibility of information and entertainment, given fabulous impetus by the inventions of this century, is relatively so recent, it would be absurd to predict with any assurance what its ultimate effects will be. But there certainly can be no doubt that business is essentially involved with the development and therefore is exerting a profound influence on the intellectual climate in which we live.

That climate, according to the hopes and beliefs that man has held in the past, should by now be unprecedently favorable to a rich, varied, and flourishing artistic accomplishment and its wide enjoyment. We should be living in a cultural golden age, for even though the American scene still has too many shameful dark corners, even though it still includes huge numbers of both urban and rural underprivileged, the over-all picture of our society is one in which wealth, leisure, and education are enjoyed on a hitherto undreamed of scale. Invention and business enterprise, capitalizing on this situation, have made art, entertainment, and information—which, throughout most of history, were available only to a select few—accessible to almost the entire population. But instead of rejoicing in our new-found cultural prosperity, most critical observers of the current scene are worried by the average quality of the material which flows out to us in such overwhelming quantity and look in vain for signs that much outstanding work is being produced.

Business pressures cannot, of course, be held solely to blame for the situation. Innumerable factors are involved. Among others, perhaps we have progressed, in our means of communicating, too rapidly for our own good, as we also seem to have done in other fields. The physical sciences have plunged forward at such a pace that we are unable to cope politically with the fruits of their invention; the vast multiplication of our school and college populations in only a few decades appears to many teachers to be at the root of the inadequacies they find in our educational apparatus and product, where we have bowed to the need to serve quantity rather than maintain the goal of producing quality.

If we are suffering in these fields from temporary stresses to which we can adjust in time, from indigestion caused by overindulgence, the problems presented are not too grim. If, on the other hand, the troubles stem from fundamental weaknesses in our systems, we are faced with far more difficult tasks.

Since mass production and mass distribution have become general in our world, the conditions governing both creative work and its dissemination have changed profoundly. In earlier times the arts and learning were usually dependent on small segments of the population, drawn mostly from the church and the aristocracy. These groups, narrow enough but at least representing intellectual leadership, comprised the arbiters of taste and the repository of knowledge. They were the only source of patronage, the sole market for artistic work, except only when the state, which was usually controlled by the same select groups, also supported creative activity.

The democratic revolutions of the eighteenth century, promising free inquiry, free speech, and general education, burst the limited horizons of earlier eras and opened new vistas for widespread participation in diversified intellectual activities. It took the fascist and communist dictatorships of our own age to reverse man's progress towards enlightenment, to deny his right not only to think for himself, but even to have independent aesthetic tastes. Under totalitarianism a rigid regimented conformity, repellent to everything modern Western man cherishes in the name of civilization, was imposed in the name of state authority by a small ruling clique.

In our own country we indignantly reject the notion of state direction or any other form of suppression and subscribe to the belief that the widest possible flow of varied uncensored output from the minds and hands of many is most to be desired. Having apparently come close to that goal in theory, we now find ourselves worried by the seeming failure of our output to measure up in practice to our high expectations. We ask with concern whether the vast expansion and the shift in the nature of communication has brought along with its benefits a leveling down of quality.

There can be no doubt that the audiences have altered radically. The attractive, the profitable markets today are made up of the bulk of the people. Our architects, for example, design factories, office buildings, and suburban developments rather than cathedrals and stately mansions for the rich. The enterprise that seeks material success sets its sights on vast numbers of potential customers. Catering to a small circle becomes more and more difficult and increasingly less likely to be a paying proposition. As the size of businesses and possibility of large profits have increased, skilled managers and promoters have more and more assumed control, earning statements and the welfare of stockholders have become matters of primary concern. In the entertainment and communication fields editorial and artistic points of view can be allowed to prevail only if they produce profitable results. Those whose job is to satisfy a large clientele are necessarily conditioned by the responses of the audience they are serving, and their own aesthetic judgments will in time be affected by the atmosphere in which they work.

This does not mean that the heads of large newspaper, magazine, book, film, radio, and television companies are evil men conforming to the radical caricaturists' pictures of them. In most cases they would like to have pride in their product and they would like to have the recognition and the regard of critical opinion that comes from making superior quality available. They usually find themselves, however, caught in a competitive situation in which not only success, but survival, demands constantly maintained or even increasing volume and allows little room either for indulging in personal tastes or in straying far from the line of proven appeal. They are also restricted by innumerable taboos, often self-imposed, designed to avoid giving offense to any substantial group and thus losing customers.

Once a structure has been created which is dependent on a given turnover, it is almost impossible to pull back. The audience exists; if one company lets some part of it get away, a rival will be there to snap it up. Film makers must provide goods that will fill huge theaters, magazines and newspapers will lose their advertising if circulation drops, sponsors demand television shows with high popularity ratings, publishers find that issuing a given twenty-five cent book is unprofitable unless it will attract close to 200,000 buyers. It does not at all follow that the article of wide circulation is necessarily inferior. The popular can, of course, be excellent and the experimental worthless. The question raised by the condition is not whether bigness in itself is good or bad, but rather whether the small can also flourish—not merely occasionally exist—alongside it. For in the field of ideas and art the new, the original, the different have always played an invaluable role. Much of what we most cherish in our intellectual heritage has in the first instance received trifling acceptance and has gradually grown and sifted down through wider and wider circles, to be appreciated eventually by large numbers. We are familiar with the stories of our most highly regarded novelists whose first several books went entirely unnoticed by the public, of great painters and musicians whose work took years to be recognized. It has been our hope that in an advancing society the obstacles to such new creative talents would diminish rather than, as we now fear, increase.

Hospitality to the original has often depended on young ambitious enterprisers trying to establish a place for themselves. We are not living in a world in which the doors are shut to such new activities, but in most fields control has become vested in fewer and fewer hands, so that competition, even though intense, is usually a struggle between giants. The cards are importantly stacked against the newcomer or the producer who is addressing himself to a small portion of the people. The newspapers with huge circulation can afford to buy innumerable features with which a less wealthy rival can scarcely compete. Book clubs and paperback editions that are based on big circulation can afford to offer bargains which make the ordinary volume of narrower appeal seem exorbitant in price. The quality magazines aimed at pleasing relatively restricted circles have to charge a much higher retail price than their mass-directed competitors, can pay far less for contributions, and can hope to have their wares on sale in only a small percentage of the localities that are available to the more popular periodicals. No one can undertake to bring a play to the commercial stage with the hope of profit unless it promises to be of hit proportions.

These conditions lead to enormous difficulties not only for the small producers, but possibly even more so for the creative artists who are as yet unrecognized or who are trying to address themselves to something less than the mass. These are apt to be the very people who explore new paths and who bring stimulation and variety to the fields in which they work. Without them conformity and repetition of proven formulas are likely to be the pattern, but at present there is evidence that the original talent which does not fit in with currently accepted popularity has tremendous difficulty in getting heard.

Even in music, where the phonograph and the radio have created an undreamed of audience for the very best and where consequently the mass distributor can make his strongest case for having contributed to cultural improvement, the young composer complains that in the midst of this musical plenty it has become no easier for the serious newcomer to get a hearing. Why should it be when so much of proven worth and popularity can be safely used?

The same problem exists in other fields. Why should one buy the work of an unknown painter when superb reproductions of great art can be had at a fraction of the cost of an original? If the classics and the most admired and best-selling contemporary authors become generally available at a very low price, who will be eager to read (or be willing to publish) the talented young who may still not have achieved their full growth and have yet to establish themselves? We cannot smugly assume that true genius will somehow find a way. The creative person normally needs the experience, the criticism, and the encouragement that comes with publication or public production.

The picture should not be painted too black. Exceptions can be found to any generalization. Unfortunately the opportunities for the unproven come too often from sources that provide limited fame and less financial nourishment. There are, for example, the learned publications, university presses, *avant-garde* magazines, little theater groups, and multitudes of amateur organizations. Our native production is also enriched and augmented by our ability to import from other parts of the world. But it is nevertheless true that the bulk of our cultural fodder is supplied by our large commercial organizations.

If businessmen in the various mass communication media are put on the defensive, they have a number of answers. They can point to enough first rate achievement to make a persuasive case. Cannot millions of people now tune in to Elmer Davis or Toscanini? Have not the movies brought Shakespeare to people to whom the living theater was never available? Are not some excellent books on sale at low cost in communities where there was never a bookstore?

If one argues that the general level is still appallingly low, they answer that even if much of the quality that they disseminate leaves a great deal to be desired, they still have made a substantial contribution in providing the great public with something which it obviously enjoys in place of the comparative emptiness that existed before. They also say that they are not responsible for the public's taste. It is up to the home and the school and the church, they claim, to educate and to raise standards. Their job is to give the public what it wants.

This is in fact much too modest a stand, for business is not merely limited to the simple role of fulfilling a demand. It also deliberately creates wants and forms habits. One need only think of the vast apparatus concerned with fashion to realize that a mighty machine works constantly to make women dissatisfied with all the clothing they already possess and to urge them to replace it. Even in more durable fields the same process goes on. The automobile industry each year tries to persuade car owners that last year's model is now quite out of date. Newspapers, radio, and television run regular features such as comic strips, soap operas, and the like, which are designed to become habit-forming. Big film producers spend fortunes to build up the glamour and the fame of stars, who are then in demand. Advertising and publicity use all their ingenuity and a great deal of money to convince people that a cigarette or a breakfast food (or even a politician) is the best of its kind and then, when they have been successful, promptly deny themselves any credit for their skill and announce triumphantly that the public has spoken. Once the verdict is in, it becomes almost heresy, or at least un-American, to suggest that the public judgment might be wrong or its taste poor. Business finds it useful to encourage the notion that what the public wants must be a good thing—an argument contradicted by the very fact that innumerable laws on the statute books are designed solely to restrict people's behavior and to keep them from indulging various of their appetites.

It is difficult to guess, in a society that has been re-shaping itself so rapidly, what the future is likely to bring. Are we at the mercy of a kind of cultural Gresham's law which says that the big (not necessarily the bad) will succeed in driving out the small (not necessarily the good)? Or are we perhaps only undergoing the growing pains of a new kind of civilization which will be formed on a much broader base of general participation from which we can expect that growing sophistication will gradually demand higher values? Even though there is so far pitifully little evidence of standards being elevated, there should be grounds for optimism in the every existence of our numerous great educational institutions and also in the interest in these problems being displayed by some of the large foundations. The present college emphasis on science and on "practical" learning may be only a temporary phase. If some of our most thoughtful educators have their way, the humanities may in time recover their traditional role as the requisite for a rounded, cultivated man. If the lively interest in creative artistic activity which exists in small circles on many of our campuses can be encouraged, strengthened, and enlarged, we may see in another generation demand from new audiences large enough to influence what big business feels it can successfully provide. It looks very much as though our best hope for higher standards depends on our institutions of learning, on their desire and their ability to produce intellectually mature citizens in sufficient numbers to be a leavening factor in the composition of the market place. For it seems certain that the conditions of the market will for a long time largely determine the kind of culture that will be available to us.

8. Educating the Uncommon Man

In American education today, we find trends that threaten not only its institutional security but its very mind and spirit. It is high time we took note of these trends. If they are allowed to continue they might easily produce an educational collapse and cultural setback from which no university could escape.

At the moment the trends show up most vividly in our schools in acute shortages of schoolrooms and teachers. But the estimates are constantly being revised upward. The latest I have at hand may be summarized as follows: In 1952–53 our total elementary school enrollment was 25,000,000 and our secondary school enrollment 6,600,000 (including, in both cases, both public and private schools). If the present rate of increase continues as expected it will give us an elementary school enrollment of between 30,000,000 and 32,000,000 by

This chapter is drawn from President Griswold's 1953 "Report to the Yale Alumni," the full text of which may be found in his newly published volume *Essays on Education,* copyright 1954 by Yale University Press.

1960, which would project itself into a secondary school enrollment of 11,000,000 to 12,000,000 by 1965. We can imagine how this in turn will swell our present higher education enrollment of around 2,000,000.

These trends have already created a shortage of classrooms which, despite our best efforts to date, stands at 325,000 and is expected to increase by another 425,000 by 1960. The results of this shortage are overcrowding, double and often triple sessions, fire and health hazards, and consequent deterioration in discipline and instruction. Far worse is the shortage of teachers. Here we discover the alarming fact that in face of the rapidly increasing enrollment of students the supply of teachers is actually declining. The projected need for properly trained and qualified elementary school teachers in the fall of 1953 was 160,000, against which our colleges produced the previous year only 36,000. To provide for a secondary school enrollment that is on its way to doubling itself we turned out 86,000 secondary school teachers in 1950; 73,000 in 1951; 61,000 in 1952; and 55,000 in 1953. "The public has been repeatedly advised," declared the 1953 Teacher Supply and Demand Report of the National Education Association, "that the American school system is rapidly moving into a new era. The facts have been literally shouted from the housetops. . . . Yet scarcely anywhere is there evidence of adequate steps being taken to meet this crisis." This arithmetic affords us only a quick barometric reading of conditions which would take another Dickens to depict and will take the best wisdom and energy this country is able to put forth to correct. Their immediate result is a nation-wide depreciation of educational standards accompanied by an inordinate waste of human resources.

On another occasion, I said that our colleges and universities depend upon the schools for their most essential raw material, and if the schools cannot or do not send them properly qualified material the whole fabric of higher education becomes a bridge built upon rotten pilings. Students who have been hustled through overcrowded and undisciplined classrooms, taught by overworked, underpaid, and improperly qualified teachers, and nurtured on subjects that do not constantly stretch their minds and expand their vision are poor material for college or university. The results of such education cannot fail to undermine the standards of both the liberal arts colleges and the graduate and professional schools of the universities. Nor have they failed to do so.

It is true that the worst effects of the trends cited above should not be felt in higher education for another decade. It was my own recent experience as a teacher in Yale College to find in my classroom each year a growing number of students who, though they might (and did) score high marks for their knowledge of the subject of the course, might have failed it altogether if I had graded them in rhetoric. Before me as I write is the annual report of the dean of one of our professional schools which complains of "widespread illiteracy among college graduates . . . want of competence effectively to read, write and spell the English language and even more to read, spell or write any foreign language . . . accordingly . . . want of capacity to acquire and apply intelligence." Beside it is a letter from a professor of economics, the distinguished graduate of European universities and former member of their faculties who has taught at both Yale and Harvard, expressing dismay at the "near illiteracy" of his graduate students in both institutions. "Few of them," he says, "know how to write, and some don't even know how to read. The main trouble undoubtedly lies with our primary and secondary education, and I am not sure how much of it could still be remedied by appropriate reforms in our undergraduate curriculum. I am afraid it may be too late by then to make up some of the deficiencies in the students' earlier training. Still, it has to be attempted. . . ." With half our graduates now entering professional schools and nearly all undergoing some form of professional or quasi-professional training after graduation, the urgency of the attempt is indicated.

I have selected this evidence from our own faculty at random. I could multiply it many times from business and industrial as well as professional and academic sources. It proves, I think, that in education as in commerce, when bad money gets into circulation it drives out good, and the process is only intensified as the latter is hoarded.

I have cited the two most obvious causes of these conditions: the shortage of facilities and the shortage of teachers. The criticism I have quoted points to a third cause, less obvious, perhaps, but certainly no less important. This is the decline of the liberal arts as a force in our national educational system. These studies are disappearing under a layer of vocational and other substitutes like the landscape in the ice age, only this glacier reaches from coast to coast and border to border. With all due exceptions, and all honor and power to those exceptions, the attitude of most educational institutions toward this trend varies from mild concern to indifference and cheerful acquiescence.

Alas, no substitutes have been found for reading and writing. The practice and enjoyment of these skills in an ever-widening orbit and on an ever-ascending plane are both ends and means to the liberal arts. If deficiencies in these skills show up in colleges and even in the highly selective graduate schools of universities, do they not betray a comprehensive deficiency of the parent discipline? At a meeting of the Association of American Universities in October, 1952, a distinguished dean from another institution, deploring the phenomenon, attributed it to the failure of the schools. I have heard school teachers blame it on the colleges. The argument moves in a vicious circle leaving untouched the central fact that both schools and colleges and through them American civilization are denying themselves the benefits of studies which, for two thousand years, throughout Western civilization, have been esteemed as the key to the good life as well as to all true academic achievement.

The point is substantiated by more disturbing evidence. While over half the nation's youth finishes high school and a fifth (of the whole) goes on to some form of higher education, this group includes less than half of those best qualified for such education. Of the top quarter in intellectual ability, 20 per cent do not continue for financial reasons, and 40 per cent—a proportion exactly equal to that which does continue—for lack of motivation.

99

That so large a proportion of our best college material eschews higher education for such a reason is a fact that requires much interpretation. It is a composite of environment, chance, social status, geography, and other elements and influences. Is it not, too, further proof of our neglect of the liberal arts? The whole impulse and tendency of the liberal arts is to encourage the individual to make the most of all educational opportunities within reach and constantly to seek new ones. If the parents and teachers of these "unmotivated" young men and women had themselves been steeped in the liberal arts would they not have communicated this impulse to their children and students? If their schools had afforded anything like proper introductions to the liberal arts, would the impulse have been lost? The voluntary rejection of higher education by so many Americans capable of profiting by it proves to my satisfaction at least that the grain cannot grow where the seed has not been planted. We can only speculate as to how much talent is wasted in the process—certainly much that would bring credit to our universities and benefit to society. This is another measure of the practical price society pays for its impractical evaluation of the liberal arts.

The prospect of "peacetime" military service, after the outbreak in Korea, whether through selective service or some form of universal military training and service showed us, no longer abstractly but concretely, the indivisible responsibility of school and college in matters of general education. Students confronted by two years in the armed forces plus four of college and three or more of professional school began to look around desperately for vocational or "pre-professional" offerings—anything that would speed up the interminable apprenticeship that stood between them and their projected careers. This, by the way, has been a universal trend, even in such traditional homes of the liberal arts as Great Britain and France. It has meant a universal setback for the liberal arts. That these countries should also be suffering from the trend is another and a compelling reason why we should take it seriously. At home it seemed as though the liberal arts were being ground between an upper millstone of vocationalism to which the weight of military service had now been added and a nether millstone of public indifference. The educational mill was grinding out skilled but uneducated human beings, American citizens who were capable but uncultivated, college graduates who were deficient in reading and writing.

There was a gap somewhere and it had to be closed. Where was it? The colleges said, in the schools. The schools said, in the colleges. Both were right. Throughout the vast majority of our secondary schools, as I have already pointed out, the liberal arts were being smothered by vocationalism. But for this the colleges were themselves partly responsible. The elective rebellion against the old liberal arts college curriculum had run wild, and colleges were giving academic credit for everything from philosophy to fly fishing. With the colleges setting such standards, how could the schools in their almost infinite diversity and their susceptibility to the moods of local boards be expected to do better? There are 75,000 public school districts in the United States, each one a highly and often pridefully autonomous community. The public high schools in these communities are attended by 92 per cent of the nation's youth enrolled in secondary education. Of the remainder, some 6 or 7 per cent attend private denominational institutions, and only 2 per cent or less private non-denominational. With this basic diversity, with only 40 per cent of the top quarter of the graduates of all these institutions sufficiently motivated to move on into any form of higher education, how could the colleges reproach the schools for neglecting Shakespeare for bookkeeping and automobile driving? What about the colleges who maintained million-dollar gate receipts by giving football players academic credit for scrimmaging and basketball players credit for rhythms and tap dancing? So the argument raged across the country, a jumble of values and standards through which the properly motivated schoolboy picked his way with all the intrepidity of the early explorers, and the universities groped for true and proper bearings.

We are confused over the very meaning of the phrase "liberal arts," let alone the subjects of study for which it stands. It has acquired connotations of special privilege and preciosity. At the risk of laboring the obvious, therefore, let us recall that, as it is used here, the word "liberal" comes from the Latin *liber*, meaning "free"; that the proper meaning of the phrase "liberal arts" is "the arts becoming to a free man"; and that from earliest times these have included the sciences (in the Middle Ages, arithmetic, geometry, and astronomy, the others being grammar, rhetoric, logic, and music). In other words the liberal arts are rooted in freedom, not privilege, and they are broad, not narrow, in educational scope.

It is true that both Greek and medieval society restricted to a minority the number of those who were truly free, hence fully qualified as beneficiaries of the arts becoming a free man. In Greek times, these were the guardians of a fundamentally undemocratic society; in medieval times, aristocrats, clergy, and wandering scholars. It is also true that this identification of the liberal arts with special orders of society dies hard in modern Britain and Europe. It grew out of a constricting interpretation of the meaning of freedom rather than a constriction inherent in the meaning of the liberal arts, and it gained currency in the United States through inverted snobbism as well as ignorance of the facts. It is as much at variance with our cardinal principle of equal opportunity as it is with the true meaning of the liberal arts.

The notion that the liberal arts are for the *rara avis* is no less difficult to explain though often more difficult to dispel. Perhaps it is attributable to the rather narrow, literal meaning our workaday society attaches to the word "arts." Thus the busy father discussing college with his son advises against "impractical" courses that will not help him in business. Or the scientist or engineer Velden stresses professional purposes with which he believes the liberal arts to be incompatible. In this the champions of the liberal arts themselves have not been altogether blameless. They have been guilty of smugness and, at times, have seemed content to live on rote and reputation.

Such, for example, appears to have been the case in British education in 1835 when Macaulay wrote in desperation, "Give a boy Robinson Crusoe. That is worth all the grammars of rhetoric and logic in the world. . . . Who ever reasoned better for having been taught the difference between a syllogism and an enthymeme? Who ever composed with greater spirit and elegance because he could define an oxymoron or an aposiopesis? I am not joking but writing quite seriously when I say that I would much rather order a hundred copies of Jack the Giant-Killer for our schools than a hundred copies of any grammar of rhetoric or logic that ever was written." The same impatience with a curriculum whose claims were pretentious but whose elements and purposes had become obscure heralded the advent of the elective system in our own schools and colleges half a century later.

All these impressions of the liberal arts rest upon a quantitative fallacy. They emphasize content as distinct from quality and spirit. If the critic reasons on this basis he may discount the liberal arts as severely as Dickens' Mr. Podsnap, who thought they should represent, reflect and conduce to "getting up at eight, shaving close at a quarter-past, breakfasting at nine, going to the City at ten, coming home at half-past five, and dining at seven. Nothing else to be permitted to those same vagrants the Arts, on pain of excommunication." Or, evidently, as their exemplars were doing when Macaulay found them exuberating in oxymorons and enthymemes and plumped for Robinson Crusoe. Or as the scientist does who forgets that science is part of the liberal arts; or the professional man who asks what Greek or Latin have to do with law or medicine or engineering.

The purpose of the liberal arts is not to teach businessmen business, or grammarians grammar, or college students Greek and Latin (which have disappeared from their required curricula). It is to awaken and develop the intellectual and spiritual powers in the individual before he enters upon his chosen career, so that he may bring to that career the greatest possible assets of intelligence, resourcefulness, judgment, and character. It is, in John Stuart Mill's telling phrase, to make "capable and cultivated human beings." "Men are men" Mill said, "before they are lawyers or physicians or manufacturers; and if you make them capable and sensible men they will make themselves capable and sensible lawyers or physicians." I know of no better statement of the purpose of the liberal arts nor any that so firmly establishes their place in a national educational system that is dedicated, as ours is, to the preparation of men and women not just for intellectual pursuits but for life.

For this statement we may proceed as Mill himself did to the conclusion that the liberal arts and many of the studies thought to be in competition with them are not competitors but allies. This was Mill's pronouncement on the conflict that raged in his day between the "old classical studies" and the "new scientific studies." Mill denied that this conflict had any foundation in principle whatsoever, declaring that "it is only the stupid inefficiency of the usual teaching which makes those studies be regarded as competitors instead of allies."

There is even less reason for such a conflict of principles today. The "old classical studies" have been greatly enriched by the infusion of history, philosophy, literature, language, and the fine arts into the erstwhile domain of the grammarian and logician. Scientific studies never were "new" to the liberal arts, as they claimed three of the original seven. The social studies—economics, anthropology, political science, sociology, psychology—have found their place in the sun alongside of language and literature. The very term "liberal arts" has given way in professional academic usage to the term "general education," with its obviously broader implications as to content and method. Every trade, profession, and vocation has an equal interest in "capable and cultivated human beings." How could this represent a conflict of principle?

It does not. The idea of a conflict of principle represents ignorance of the facts with its usual by-products of misunderstanding and prejudice. That this is so should give us courage to attack these ancient enemies of learning. But where do we begin? With the conditions cited at the beginning of this report—the overcrowded schoolrooms, the shortage of teachers? What can the universities do about them? Could we not turn our backs on them and count on our reputations to bring us our quota of exceptional or specially privileged individual students? Quite apart from its morality when viewed in the light of our charters, our aims and ideals as national universities, and our tax-exempt status, such a policy would surely defeat itself. We have seen how the general deterioration of educational standards is already being felt in our undergraduate and professional schools. To turn our backs on this would be to court disaster. For our own sake as well as for the country's we must face it and do something about it.

We must and we can. Though we cannot produce a magic formula that will relieve the shortages of schoolrooms and teachers, we can do a number of things that will contribute to those results. Above all I would name two: First, we can maintain the liberal arts in the fullest possible health and vigor in the universities, and second, we can capitalize them as a motivating force in American education by improving and expanding our liberal arts training program for secondary school teachers. Both steps would lead directly to improved conditions in the schools as well as in the universities. For of this I am convinced: that if this country is to be shaken out of the trance that blinds it to the needs of its educational system, the great awakening will be brought about by parents and teachers steeped in the liberal arts and imbued with their spirit. It is both the duty and the opportunity of the American universities to make this experience rich and fruitful for their own students and, through them, to bring this spirit powerfully to the assistance of American education.

9. The Common Man on the Campus

WHAT is or should be the relation of the American university to the cultural scene today? (And—for convenience—I include in the word "university" the whole panorama of higher education.) That it has a responsibility would seem to be beyond argument.

For many years professional mourners have been wailing—with a good deal of reason—about "the decline of the humanities." The kind of world we have created and the values by which it continues to try to exist have not been kind to the gentler spirit of man. Merely to survive, at whatever level, would seem to take all the energy and imagination of which we are capable. It is a strange comment on our civilization that the really life-giving forces which stand for the dignity of man, the beauty of human life, and the richness of the human spirit should have to be defended as if they were something peripheral to the really important business of the modern world—a sort of hole-and-corner activity suitable enough as a social adornment, a graceful adjunct to getting on, an acceptable employment for those hours of leisure when everyone, with his social security pension in his pocket, will curl up in the chimney corner with a good book. Because that is so clearly not what the humanities mean it is a pleasure to come to their defense, believing that what we lightly call civilization has reached a kind of crossroad and is in danger of being swamped by its own gigantic stupidities. We need to be reminded that spiritual toughness and resiliency are just as important, if not more important, than mechanical achievement. The humanities, far from being an escape from life, can be a stay to us in the crises of life.

Too often, however, the universities have become a repository for the humanities rather than their interpreter in the broad stream of American culture. Part of this failure stems from the fact that scientific man is the popular hero today. "Knowledge comes, but wisdom lingers," Tennyson put it; the wistful professor of the arts and literatures watches the linear accelerators and the cyclotrons grow in multiple-million-dollar grandeur at the heart of the campus while the library and the art gallery struggle along on emaciating diets. To the extent that mechanical efficiency and production are the integrating factors of our civilization, the universities merely reflect the chief concerns of society. Electronics is God.

It is true that the real education of our time proceeds for the most part outside academic halls. Much of it takes place for the youngster before he starts to school. And later, for many, the mass media take over. It is perhaps too much to ask the ablest professor to accomplish what parents have been unable to do, and to regenerate the human spirit in a short series of fifty-minute sessions. One suspects that many of the concepts of what constitutes real happiness in life, or what constitutes real success, for example, have been pretty much formed by the time the freshman matriculates.

Yet beyond this the practitioners of the humanities must themselves accept some responsibility for the unwillingness to accept what they purvey. Too frequently they fail to make viable for their students the great cultural heritage of which they are the custodians. Young people need desperately to discover the enduring greatness inherent in the human record and to learn from that record sympathy and understanding and a knowledge of the great compelling forces that have distinguished and dignified mankind. Too many professors are content merely to botanize upon the grave of the humanities. Without decision themselves, they reflect endlessly, but never get beyond the stage of intellectual shadow-boxing. To deal with life and yet to render it sterile is the unforgivable academic crime. Somehow the great ideas must be made to come alive for the student in his contemporary context.

To that extent, then, the humanistic studies have declined and have failed to affect the stream of modern life; the causes are complex, partly within and partly without the university. A recurrent nightmare for any professor is one in which he finds himself asking a former student what he has read since graduation. And that which the professor fears to ask is now being dragged into the light by such people as Dr. George Gallup and his associates, with terrifying results.

Undoubtedly the true function of the university is to stimulate to excellence, to encourage in the Age of the Common Man the Uncommon Man to whom Mr. Krutch referred in an earlier essay. Its first job, therefore, is to do well that for which it was created. Has it any responsibility beyond this to a larger public, any obligation to shape and improve American taste at different levels outside the area of its immediate clientele? Is it a social force in the large? And is it even understood by the public upon which it depends, in the long run, for support?

Recent events would seem to show that the function of the university, beyond its capacity to train people in the professions or to give them a set of trade-techniques, is dimly comprehended by the public at large. This has been clearly evident in the controversies about loyalty oaths for university faculties: the very bases of intellectual freedom, without which the university loses its essential character, have seemed to the man in the street just a set of long-haired shibboleths. No wonder that unscrupulous politicians have been quick to capitalize on this ignorance for their own ends. Much of the fault lies with the universities themselves. Either they have taken for granted that the necessity for their freedoms has been self-evident, or somewhat arrogantly declined to descend from their mountain and explain it to the *hoi polloi*. And then they wonder why they get a bad press!

From the larger cultural point of view what responsibility does the university have to the public, particularly as concerns a possible influence on the mass media? Here the history of the university as it was faced by radio is instructive. In a few instances intelligent and careful university planning produced programs of real quality, which have continued to live because they deserved to. More frequently, however, the university, ignorant of the terrific weapon which, for good or bad, lay at hand, took a haughty attitude toward a medium which clearly was not at the moment being used chiefly for the public enlightenment. Occasionally the radio stations, with the Federal Communications Commission breathing down their necks, would offer educational time. And occasionally the university would deign to put its professors on the air—usually in a series of half-hour lectures originally designed for the captive audience in the classroom. No one should have been surprised that radio sets clicked off all over the land, or that the stations later withdrew the time and offered it to hillbilly bands.

The case of television is somewhat different. Because it is so new to the educational world it is still pretty much an unknown quantity. Even the most conservative of educators has recognized the terrific impact of television and has caught a glimpse of its potential uses. Witness the scramble for unallocated educational channels. Here too one wonders if all the implications have been faced: financial, technical, programmatic. Yet even apart from the new channels, the commercial companies (still FCC conscious) are eager to offer a modest portion of their facilities for educational purposes. The danger now is not that the universities will scorn such offers, but rather that they will rush in to muddy the air-waves with inferior programs, and thus destroy their amazing opportunity to reach the public which so much needs to understand them. For television is not radio, nor is it the classroom lectern. Its proper educational use will require time and careful preparation—in university budgetary terms: money. Properly utilized, its potential is incalculable; unimaginatively used, it will be just another proof that universities should stay on the campus.

While concentrating on its main job, the university does have a secondary but by no means minor responsibility to raise the cultural level of the society which feeds it—or at the very least to be sensitively concerned that the level of the "common" man should be lifted to the extent of his capacities. No university can be culturally healthy in a culturally sick society. Yet the primary task of the university is still the training in wisdom (which means more than knowledge) of those who are told, every Commencement, that they are to be leaders. To the extent that the universities have defaulted and are turning out technicians in a variety of intellectual skills—men who lack the human understanding which will give them a wisdom of choice and a basis for constructive action commensurate with their technical ability—to that extent higher education is merely compounding the confusion of our times, and giving it weapons with which to destroy itself. Culture, in its deepest sense, is moral as well as intellectual and esthetic. In its broader significance it may well mark the difference between extinction and survival.

10. Let's Globalize Our Universities

AMERICAN education is having trouble adjusting to the swiftness and the magnitude of the change in our world position. This is true even though a capacity for adjustment and innovation has been a special characteristic of American higher education. The commonest criticism of universities in this country by foreign visitors is that they have been too responsive to the needs of society. This, it is said, has caused a dilution of standards and a dispersion of effort. British universities have been relatively insensitive to their environment to the extent that major reforms have often been the results of pressures and demands arising outside the British university system. Changing the curriculum in British universities is a little like moving a graveyard.

The humanities are not paying enough attention to the history, intellectual activity, influence, and experience of the new magnitudes and multitudes of China, India, the Arab world, which today intimately confront American life. This means bluntly that there is in the

114

light of the needs of America today a disproportionate preoccupation with the history, the intellectual activity, the influence and experience of Western Europe. I am raising a question which can only be controversial.

This is not a plea for more teaching of current events. We are already exposed enough to the danger of capriciously devising new courses and programs of instruction to meet the fluctuations of politics, economics, or art. This is a plea that a resolute effort be made to correct our dangerous illiteracy in the life and thought of great areas of the world where history has begun to roll at such a pace that the things on which we place the greatest value—our security, our way of life, our economic stability—are intimately affected.

Illiteracy in science and technology is much less dangerous for the citizen of a democracy than illiteracy in history or politics or morality. We can drive an automobile across the George Washington Bridge without knowing much about the scientific principles that govern the motor or the engineering principles that govern the bridge. If necessary we can buy the services of trained experts when something goes wrong. But in our role as citizens we must have a substantial degree of personal expertness. There is an indispensable minimum of knowledge, of direct participation and individual judgment, that cannot be delegated. Such delegation is the first step toward the abandonment of democracy itself. Whether the transfer of power and initiative in our stupendous age will take place without a major disaster, or whether we are about to plunge into a catastrophe more cruel than the sum of those we have now twice endured, it is clear that our ignorance will give us little chance of influencing the revolution that has spilled into most of the world.

It would mean a great step toward basic wisdom if we could remove enough of this illiteracy so that a secretary of state could recognize the inappropriateness of presenting General Naguib with a pistol for his "defense" at a moment when Egypt all at the same time is quarreling with Great Britain, Israel, and embarking on difficult internal reforms. How many of the politicians, editors, and generals who speak and write with influence on our Eastern policy have pondered and absorbed some of the economic and human meaning of the following sentences from Maurice Zinkin's recent book?: "The most bankrupt countryside in Asia is China. The worst crisis of overpopulation China has yet had to face has been accompanied by a breakdown of traditional ideas and traditional authority so complete as to lead to a state of near anarchy." It is surely hardly possible to act or speak sensibly on any matter affecting our relations with China without taking into account the economic agony of 500,000,000 people. How many people have a good enough acquaintance with the history and thought of India to understand the neutralism of Mr. Nehru, which controls the balance of power in Asia, or to discern the possible truth in the assertion that the capital event of our generation may well be, not the antithesis of Russia and the United States, but the coming effort of a liberal India and a Communist China to solve the same momentous problems of poverty, disease, underequipment, debt, landlessness, overpopulation, ignorance, by the use of very different economic and political principles and procedures? How many people see that the search for power in the Middle East or Africa is also a search of dignity and self-respect? How many of us know enough of the needs of Africa and Asia to mourn over the pity and the waste that America, one of the great frontier societies of history, should have to transform itself into a great military power, when its experience in conquering want and disease could be at work helping on the new frontiers of the earth to create the longer years of human life that Americans enjoy?

America's consciousness of its world must undergo the same transformation that occurred in Western Europe in the sixteenth and seventeenth centuries as a result of the great voyages of discovery. The knowledge of new places and peoples, beliefs and practices, crowded upon Europe's consciousness. Paul Hazard called it *"La crise dans la conscience européenne."* Truths that had seemed absolute became relative; beliefs that were assured became doubtful. Large new bodies of information had to be incorporated. Discrepancies between ideas, and collisions between beliefs, had to be reconciled and mediated. The outcome was an enlargement of horizons, an expansion of knowledge, and a new view of the world without which Western Europe could not have moved into its new position of world leadership.

To a degree that we do not yet recognize, with an unparalleled speed, we are discovering a new world. We are under a compulsion, too great to exaggerate, to develop an effective consciousness of the new world which is arising. Between us and it there is no effective sea-power to reduce our involvement, no stable colonial relationships to control or direct the pace of historic change. There is really not a buffer or screen left between us and the world. In this need for a new consciousness of the world there is what the Germans call *Notwendigkeit,* a compulsion at the same time inevitable and indispensable. By remaining ignorant and illiterate we are simply multiplying the chances of being wrong in a big way in our relations with a world in revolution.

Our educational habits and practices have of necessity been deeply influenced by Western Europe. We are an extension of Western Europe. It is there that are the the roots of our law, religion, government, and much else. There are big guns that can be brought up to defend the place in the curriculum of the literature, the history, and the art of the different epochs and countries of Western Europe. Some of the subjects they defend are vital and could never be given up. Yet there simply must be room in general education, in the undergraduate curriculum, in the basic instruction of the 2,500,000 students in college, for the opportunity to bring into focus the new world which, if you please, the collapse of Western Europe has produced.

It is true that many of the larger universities have shown considerable enterprise in developing institutes for the specialized study of China, the Middle East, and India. Usually they cater to the training of a few specialists, and otherwise live in their own enclaves inside the main body of the curriculum. There they are treated with a sort of neutral politeness by the rest of the faculty,

and provided with enough of the appearances of co-
operation to keep the foundations happy. In any case
these institutes have largely joined the trend of the graduate schools towards specialization, and away from the
broad learning of the good liberal arts curriculum. There
is something to be gained, but not enough, in permitting
a few more students to view the world through the eye
of a needle held by an Arabist or Sinologist. Only an unusual effort, backed by real vision and real courage, will
bring about the reassessment of the undergraduate curriculum which is required to ease what Paul Hazard today would call *"La crise dans la conscience américaine."*
Reassessment means broadening, not the addition of
new specialties; not to see people through the eye of a
needle, but to gain a perception of their nature, the flowering of their art, their answers to the problems of good
and evil, their careers amid the great forces of climate
and history, their hopes for the future. It means a re-
spectful making of room, even at the expense of conden-
sation or restriction elsewhere, to enable students to
learn some fundamental things about several billion very
important human beings. This means less room and time
in an undergraduate curriculum for the subjects and
materials which are drawn from the nations of Western
Europe. Or, better still, it means a skillful selection of
what cannot be sacrificed. Of this there is still much.

The nations of Western Europe are finding it hard
to accept the realities of their reduced stature in the
modern world. When Churchill proposed last May that
a high-level conference with the Soviet Union be held,
"confined to the smallest number of powers and persons

possible," irritation ran high in Paris for fear that France might not be ranked among the few great powers. It is not hard to see that the greatest single problem in American foreign policy is to determine the place which Western Europe must hold in the new system of America's world relationships. In Iran, Egypt, Indonesia, Southeast Asia, China, and Africa, American foreign policy has since 1945 been continuously trying, clumsily and empirically, to establish a scale of diplomatic, strategic, and human values between old empires and new peoples. Ultimately the new values and proportions will be established in our foreign policy, as they will in the college curriculum. Can they be established soon enough and effectively enough? History is ahead of schedule. Events which we vaguely assumed in my college days might happen toward the end of the century are happening right now. The great thunder of their consequence is already on the horizon. We cannot escape the sensation of the concentration and speeding up of events which Europe felt after Columbus and Luther; and which the habits and practices of slower paced generations had difficulty overtaking. A Zulu mineworker once collided heavily with me as he dashed down a Johannesburg road towards the railroad depot. "Ha! Sorry, Baas," he said, "time is few!" and dashed off to catch his train. In Asia and Africa, time is few, very few.

It is of the greatest importance that we do not see the new materials or courses which are here recommended as simple additions or replacements. Unless they are also seen and accepted as a new ferment, a new modifying substance within our intellectual environment, they will do no more than crowd the curriculum and irritate faculties. A penetrating understanding of Russian history is at the same time a revision of American history. To bring the religion or philosophy or economics of Asia into our intellectual consciousness is to modify all else within that consciousness. It is in part a rewriting of American history to be forced to recognize, as I am sure we honestly must, that the most important ally the Soviet Union has had in its unsettlement of the colonial relations of the modern world has been the United States. At this moment of tragic confrontation it is a blow to recognize that the anticolonialism which was bred of the American revolution involuntarily joined forces with Leninist antiimperialism to erode the already weakening foundation of Western Europe's colonial systems. (The same factors have a responsibility for creating the power vacuums in the Middle East, Southeast Asia, Germany, and elsewhere, each of which, to change the figure, can become the trigger of war.) This is a revision of American history that could lead us to look with greater tolerance and understanding upon the individuals whom we are now ignobly blaming for the collapse of our relations with China. We might learn that the industrial and economic procedures that give us power and security will, for a very long season, be a brutal upheaval in the lives of the unscientific, superstitious peasantries of the earth, and that even without communism there is bound to be new radicalism on the face of the earth.

Education in a democracy is a form of statesmanship which seeks a wise middle course between participation and isolation. One reason for the existence of universities is to provide an intellectual refuge for those who know how to honor and reward the privilege. But there are periods when the compulsion towards participation is strong. A merely passive spectatorship of our uneasy world is unethical. The humanities today cannot be a shelter from the world of action. If scholars refuse to admit this they must not be unhappy if the world of action ignores them.

11. Seek the Finer Flavor

THERE are forces at large in our society today that are too diffuse to be described by their association with the name of any one man or any one political concept.

They have no distinct organizational forms. They are as yet largely matters of the mind and the emotion in large masses of individuals. But they all march, in one way or another, under the banner of an alarmed and exercised anti-communism—but an anti-communism of a quite special variety, bearing an air of excited discovery and proprietorship, as though no one had ever known before that there was a communist danger; as though no one had ever thought about it and taken its measure; as though it had begun about the year 1945 and these people were the first to learn of it.

I have no quarrel to pick with the ostensible purpose of the people in which these forces are manifest. Surely, many of them are sincere. Surely, many of them have come to these views under real provocation and out of real bewilderment. But I have the deepest misgivings about the direction and effects of their efforts.

In general, I feel that what they are doing is unwise and unfortunate, and I am against it. They distort and exaggerate the dimensions of the problems with which they profess to deal. They confuse internal and external aspects of the communist threat. They insist on portraying as contemporary realities things that had their actuality years ago. They insist on ascribing to the workings of domestic communism evils and frustrations which, in so far as they were not part of the normal and unavoidable burden of complexity in our life, were the product of our behavior generally as a nation, and should today be the subject of humble and contrite soul-searching on the part of all of us, in a spirit of brotherhood and community, rather than of frantic and bitter recrimination.

And having thus incorrectly stated the problem, it is no wonder that these people constantly find the wrong answers. They tell us to remove our eyes from the constructive and positive purposes and to pursue with fanaticism the negative and vindictive ones. They sow timidity where there should be boldness; fear where there should be serenity; suspicion where there should be confidence and generosity. In this way they impel us—in the name of our salvation from the dangers of communism—to many of the habits of thought and action which our Soviet adversaries, I am sure, would most like to see us adopt and which they have tried unsuccessfully over a period of some thirty-five years to graft upon us through the operations of their Communist party.

These forces are narrowly exclusive in their approach to our world position, and carry this exclusiveness vigorously into the field of international cultural exchanges. They tend to stifle the interchange of cultural impulses that is vital to the progress of the intellectual and artistic life of our people. The people in question seem to feel either that cultural values are not important at all or that America has reached the apex of cultural achievement and no longer needs in any serious way the stimulus of normal contact with other peoples in the field of arts and letters.

They look with suspicion both on the sources of intellectual and artistic activity in this country and on impulses of this nature coming to us from abroad. The remote pasts of foreign artists and scholars are anxiously scanned before they are permitted to enter our land, and this is done in proceedings so inflexible in concept and offensive in execution that their very existence often constitutes a discouragement to cultural interchange. The personal movements and affairs of great scholars and artists are thus passed upon and controlled by people who have no inkling of understanding for the work these same scholars and artists perform.

In this way, we begin to draw about ourselves a cultural curtain similar in some respects to the Iron Curtain of our adversaries. In doing so, we tend to inflict upon ourselves a species of cultural isolation and provincialism wholly out of accord with the traditions of our nation and destined, if unchecked, to bring to our intellectual and artistic life the same sort of sterility from which the cultural world of our Communist adversaries is already suffering.

Within the framework of our society, as in its relations to external environment, the tendency of these forces is exclusive and intolerant—quick to reject, slow to receive, intent on discovering what ought not to be rather than what ought to be. They claim the right to define a certain area of our national life and cultural output as beyond the bounds of righteous approval. This definition is never effected by law or by constituted authority; it is effected by vague insinuation and suggestion. And the circle, as I say, tends to grow constantly narrower. One has the impression that, if uncountered, these people would eventually narrow the area of political and cultural respectability to a point where it included only themselves, the excited accusers, and excluded everything and everybody not embraced in the profession of denunciation.

I recall reading recently, twice in one day, the words of individuals who proclaimed that if certain other people did not get up and join actively in the denunciation of Communists or communism, they would thereby themselves be suspect. What sort of arrogance is this? Every one of us has his civic obligations. Every one of us has his moral obligations to principles.

I am not condoning anyone for forgetting these obligations. But to go beyond this—to say that it is not enough to be a law-abiding citizen—to say that we all have some obligation to get up and make statements of this tenor or that with respect to other individuals, or else submit to being classified as suspect in the eyes of our fellow citizens—to assert this is to establish a new species of public ritual, to arrogate to one's individual self the powers of the spiritual and temporal law-giver, to make the definition of social conduct a matter of fear in the face of vague and irregular forces, rather than a matter of confidence in the protecting discipline of conscience and the law.

I have lived more than ten years of my life in totalitarian countries. I know where this sort of thing leads. I know it to be the most shocking and cynical disservice one can do to the credulity and to the spiritual equilibrium of one's fellow men. And this sort of thing cannot fail to have its effect on the liberal arts, for it is associated with two things that stand in deepest conflict to the development of mind and spirit: with a crass materialism and anti-intellectualism on the one hand, and with a marked tendency toward a standardization and conformity on the other.

In these forces I have spoken about, it seems to me that I detect a conscious rejection and ridicule of intellectual effort and distinction. They come together here with a deep-seated weakness in the American character: a certain shy self-consciousness that tends to deny interests other than those of business, sport, or war.

There is a powerful strain of our American cast of mind that has little use for the artist or the writer, and professes to see in the pursuits of such people a lack of virility—as though virility could not find expression in the creation of beauty, as though Michelangelo had never wielded his brush, as though Dante had never taken up his pen, as though the plays of Shakespeare were lacking in manliness. The bearers of this neomaterialism seem, indeed, to have a strange self-consciousness about the subject of virility—a strange need to emphasize and demonstrate it by exhibitions of taciturnity, callousness, and physical aggressiveness—as though there were some anxiety lest, in the absence of these exhibitions, it might be found wanting.

What weakness is it in us Americans that so often makes us embarrassed or afraid to indulge the gentle impulse to seek the finer and rarer flavor, to admit frankly and without stammering apologies to an appreciation for the wonder of the poet's word and the miracle of the artist's brush, for all the beauty, in short, that has been recorded in the images of word and line created by the hands of men in past ages? What is it that makes us fear to acknowledge the greatness of other lands, or of other times, to shun the subtle and the unfamiliar?

What is it that causes us to huddle together, herd-like, in tastes and enthusiasms that represent only the common denominator of popular acquiescence, rather than to show ourselves receptive to the tremendous flights of creative imagination of which the individual mind has shown itself capable? Is it that we are forgetful of the true sources of our moral strength, afraid of ourselves, afraid to look into the chaos of our own breasts, afraid of the bright, penetrating light of the great teachers?

This fear of the untypical, this quest for security within the walls of secular uniformity—these are traits of our national character we would do well to beware of and to examine for their origins. They receive much encouragement these days, much automatic and un-intended encouragement, by virtue of the growing standardization of the cultural and, in many respects, the educational influences to which our people are being subjected.

The immense impact of commercial advertising and the mass media on our lives is—let us make no mistake about it—an impact that tends to encourage passivity, to encourage acquiescence and uniformity, to place handicaps on individual contemplativeness and creativeness. It may not seem to many of us too dangerous that we should all live, dress, eat, hear, and read substantially alike. But we forget how easily this uniformity of thought and habit can be exploited, when the will to exploit it is there. We forget how easily it can slip over into the domination of our spiritual and political lives by self-appointed custodians who contrive to set themselves at the head of popular emotional currents.

There is a real and urgent danger here for anyone who values the right to differ from others in any manner whatsoever, be it in his interests or his associations or his faith. There is no greater mistake we of this generation can make than to imagine that the tendencies which in other countries have led to the nightmare of totalitarianism will, as they appear in our midst, politely pause—out of some delicate respect for American tradition—at the point where they would begin to affect our independence of mind and belief.

The forces of intolerance and political demagoguery are greedy forces, and unrestrained. There is no limit to their ambitions or their impudence. They contain within themselves no mechanism of self-control. Like the ills of Pandora's box, once released, they can be stopped only by forces external to themselves. The only permanent thing behind them all is still the naked vulnerable, human soul, the scene of the age-old battle between good and evil, assailed with weakness and imperfections, always in need of help and support, and yet sometimes capable of such breath-taking impulses of faith and creative imagination.

Finally, it lies with the devotees of the liberal arts to combat the forces of intolerance in our society: to convince people that these forces are incompatible with the flowering of the human spirit, to remember that the ultimate judgments of good and evil are not ours to make: that the wrath of man against his fellow man must always be tempered by the recollection of his weakness and fallibility and by the example of forgiveness and redemption which is the essence of his Christian heritage.

12. The Taste of the Common Man

I T is not very long since the U.S. Post Office (and other learned and religious institutions) celebrated the fifth centenary of the Gutenberg Bible. We all learned at school what a great event that was, how inestimably beneficent the invention of printing had been. From it, the Victorian orators could declaim, how much good had come, above all the unexampled progress of the modern world. We are not, in these days of the hydrogen bomb, quite so enamored of our unexampled progress and we are not even enamored of all the results of printing, leaving atomic physics on one side. As it happened, I had to go to London to broadcast on the first Sunday of my return to Britain and visiting a friend was able to renew my acquaintance with the most popular newspaper in Britain, not only in Britain but in the world. For *The News of the World* sells 7,000,000 copies every Sunday, this in a population of fifty millions! And it is a safe bet that, five hundred years after the first printed Bible, more Britons have for their Sabbath reading *The News of the World* than the Bible. Such has been the progress of popular culture! And, this is the point I want to make, that progress has been the same in Britain as in the United States; as mere literacy has spread, so apparently have taste, decency, and the power of reflection diminished.

I have begun with the case of *The News of the World* to show that we are dealing with a universal phenomenon, for the staples of that great journal are sex and crime (if the two are combined, so much the better) and sport, closely associated, of course, for this is England, with gambling. When the pessimistic American luxuriates in the gloomy thoughts bred by contemplating American popular taste, let him take comfort; he is not alone. All over the modern world, the same problem is with us. Can a democratic and egalitarian culture have what previous generations of the literate called culture? Is there a Gresham's law in this field as in currency? Must barbarity drive out civilization?

That the phenomenon is universal is easily enough illustrated from the immense vogue of American films, comics, popular music, and "tough" novels; from the popularity of the American Forces Network; from the crowds that mob Danny Kaye and Frank Sinatra; from the Americanization of Paris and Rome as well as London and Edinburgh. Modern industrial society, with the immensely improved technical facilities for diffusion of music, literature, ideas, and fads that science has provided, has made possible, for the first time, the diffusion of the same music, literature, ideas, fads all over the Western world. From the rigorous denunciations that come from the Soviet and satellite press, one may suspect that it is only the Iron Curtain that saves the masses of the People's Democracies from the contagion of the New World's quick stain.

There are, that is to say, no fundamental differences in the problem of popular taste in Europe and in America, at any rate, in the industrialized parts of Europe and America. An illiterate Spanish shepherd in Estremadura may still know no songs but the old ballads, but that is because Spain is backward. As she moves forward, she will, despite the traditional gravity and dignity of the Spaniard, run into bebop and the comics. We are all in the same boat together, or in the same kind of boats, for the American boat is bigger and better. But it is not fundamentally different.

What is the boat or boats that we are in? Our situation has been admirably described, in its American context, by Joseph Wood Krutch and by others. We are the first civilization in which the canons of taste are laid down by the majority of the inhabitants of a civilization that has largely had its roots with its traditional culture cut and is busy manufacturing a new culture, with a speed and universality that modern technology alone makes possible. We have the masses and the mass media; two significant phenomena and two significant names.

And, as in everything else in this Western industrialized world, the lead comes from the United States. There can be found the greatest masses, the most developed mass media, and—as far as it is a question of supply and demand—the greatest seller's market. If it were only by its size, the American problem of popular taste would

be the crucial problem, for America is by her economic
and military power a world leader. The led (French,
English, Germans, Italians) have only a limited power
of resistance and have a natural interest in the trend of
American taste and in the nature of American exploitation of the technical miracles of communication.

But it is not only the scale of American emission of
books and comics and music and dancing that marks it
off from Europe. It is the color of the society that produces these artifacts. For it is true that in many, perhaps
in most, ways America is socially more egalitarian, more
impatient of traditional authority than even revolutionary or socialist societies in Europe. For in Europe, over
the revolutionary, over the radical, over even the Communist hangs the pall of the past. The great monuments
are not tributes to the sovereign people, least of all the
Kremlin. There is visible everywhere a past in which
leadership, in all aspects of life, was in the hands of a
confident, accepted, and obeyed minority, kings and
nobles, priests, princes and merchant princes. Universities and academies, schools and museums all speak of
the past, the not-very-remote past, when the poor, as
an Anglican bishop put it, had nothing to do with the
laws but to obey them.

Among the laws to be obeyed were the laws of taste.
The republic of letters was no more a modern democratic republic than were the slave-based republics of
Athens or Rome. And, although this is a platitude, it is
one worth insisting on. If there is a crisis of American
taste, it is an aspect of that most important quality of
American life, the feeling of the American "new man"

that he is as good as anybody and better than most. There is not only in America an older and deeper tradition of equality, of all opinions, and all people running a race for visible, tangible primacy, there have been and still are no impossible ambitions. From a log cabin in Kentucky, from the wrong side of the tracks in Kansas to the White House is a way trodden by Presidents in 1861 and today. From Fisherman's Wharf in San Francisco to supremacy on the baseball diamond, from the Negro slums of Detroit to the boxing championship of the world, there are careers open to all talents and measured in the same way—popularity, power, money or all three. There are no inaccessible heights, like the throne in England, no closed corporations that the average man really cares much about, no Académie Francaise, no hierarchy of academic or professional talents from Professor Ordinarius to Sanitätsrat.

And there is nowhere the permanent action of the state in setting norms, in rewarding talent, in classing talents. There is no Order of Merit, no Order of Lenin. If there were an Order of Merit in America, what administration would dare to ignore public opinion in awarding it? (The history of the Bollingen Prize suggests an answer.) The artist, the musician, the author must compete unaided, not only with Joe DiMaggio and Joe Louis, with Danny Kaye and Marilyn Monroe, he must compete in his own field with the star artists of *The Saturday Evening Post*, with the star writers of *The Reader's Digest*, resist the temptations of Hollywood and the seductions of the book clubs. The wonder is not that there is so much vulgar, trivial stuff on the air, on television, on the newsstands, but that there is anything else.

But despite these important institutional differences, I repeat, the problem is, at bottom, the same in Paris and in London as it is in New York and Los Angeles. The problem is distorted, hidden by the survival of an aristocratic culture, by the survival of aristocratic institutions. Even when those institutions—the Académie Francaise, the Royal Academy—have lost most of their prestige among the very classes they are supposed to represent and lead, they keep it (for the time being at any rate) among the less literate and less culturally sophisticated. If we assume for the moment (possibly un-American thought) that there are standards not identical with those of mass popular appeal, the American David is smaller and less well-armed, the American Goliath bigger and more formidable than their European counterparts. There are Philistines everywhere, but American Philistines are bigger and better. Bigger, which goes without saying, and better—as all the world proves by its lavish flattery of imitation. If the average American is fit to choose presidents and judges, he is fit to choose artists and musicians, and he does choose them by the most effective means possible, by paying for them.

There is another, more accidental aspect of the American cultural democracy, the absence of a cultural capital. New York may be that more than it was, but New York, even if it has replaced—as a literary and publishing center—Boston, Philadelphia, Chicago, and San Francisco, is still not a center of national cultural life like Paris or London. It has to compete, still, with its old rivals, with Hollywood, even a little possibly with Washington! There cannot be a unified identifiable class of cultural leaders such as there can be in Paris or London. There cannot even be rival unified groups, in close proximity and in competition. The existence of such groups may not be healthy but they make possible the imposition of a lead, if only a lead by snobbery, on publishing, on the stage, on the BBC, and on the Radio-Diffusion Francaise. The kind of public opinion that makes possible the Third Program, with its handful of listeners, does not exist and could not exist in America, even if radio were a government monopoly. What we call, or used to call, "high culture" has to fight for its life in America without the usual aids it has in Europe. (It has aids it hasn't got in Europe, but that is a story I'll come to later.)

Then there is a modern phenomenon in American life that may be passing and that I hope and think is passing, what I shall call "egalitarian nationalism." This takes the form of asserting or implying that there is something fresh, new, admirable in the most popular successes that gives them a claim on our attention equal to that of what we used to call masterpieces. It is smart, for the smart, to make a jazz improviser equal to Schnabel, or Gershwin equal to Richard Strauss. And these assertions are made, not only because these popular art forms are popular, but because they are American. In the theatrical passion for the American past, if it is no further back than *Miss Liberty* or *Oklahoma!*, there is, I am sure a nostalgia for the older, more secure, more innocent, and— we assume, without proof—happier days of our fathers.

This affection of the eggheads (then known as high-brows) for the "seven lively arts" had a good deal of justification when Gilbert Seldes launched the phrase and the crusade. America was just emerging from the grasp of the genteel tradition. Pressed against the flat and rigid bosom of academic taste, the lusty young *enfants terribles* of the first postwar period were ready to do anything to escape from the schoolmarms, the dominies, the National Academy of Arts and Letters. There were the movies, there was jazz!; while the last vapid runnings of the not very strong New England brew were being issued to the no longer docile young. It was better to plug *The Garrick Gaieties* than read the works of the epigoni of Emerson or Howells. The era of beautiful nonsense talked a lot of nonsense and this was part of it but it was only partly nonsense. Today it is much more like a *trahison des clercs*.

This is not to say that there is not a great deal to be said for many popular successes. Compare the better musical of today with the imbecile "musical comedies" of a generation ago. Compare, if it comes to that, *Kiss Me Kate* with Shakespeare's botched job! *Oklahoma!* may turn out to be a permanent minor classic like the best of Gilbert and Sullivan. Some tunes from other shows may have the lesser immortality of Stephen Foster. But "I'm Gonna Wash that Man" isn't "Take O Take Those Lips Away"; *South Pacific* isn't *The Marriage of Figaro* or even *Der Rosenkavalier,* and neither *The Member of the Wedding* nor *A Streetcar* is *Othello* or *Le Misanthrope*. Indeed, the new democratic snobbery makes the very real merits, the serious and permanent merits of a play like *The Member of the Wedding* appear less than they are, since Shakespeare and Miss Mc-Cullers are both less popular, less "democratic" than the people who write and produce "I Love Lucy." If there are no standards other than popular appeal, then we know where we are. There's no business like box office and a high rating or a record booking recorded in *Variety*.

It is against this background that we have to consider the level of the American mass media (and I include much more than radio and movies in that term; I mean the comics; I mean the paperback books; I mean the less eminent magazines you find in the drugstore). I think there is, in the first place, too much moaning over the generally low quality of the products of all these industries. Masterpieces, even second-class masterpieces, are rare; and if you are to keep on issuing new stuff all the time, much of it is bound to be poor, like much of the Elizabethan drama, like most of the immense French drama. As long as you don't confuse soap opera with Mozart or Wagner, no great harm is done, and I can see little difference in nonintellectual content between British and American soap opera.

Much of the mere entertainment on the air and on the screen does not entertain sophisticated people. Some of it does; but because I am not continuously amused by Mr. Sid Caesar or Miss Imogene Coca this does not mean that they are not amusing, or that people who are amused by them every time they appear on the screen are either fools or even conspicuously wasting their time. That depends on what they would be doing with their time if they weren't viewing. That there is too much violence on the air and on the screen and in the movies I do not doubt. But there is too much violence in American life. Does anyone think that if the BBC took over the American radio and television business, the New York docks would become a nest of singing birds? If people can believe that Mr. Anastasia and his friends are the products of the mass media, they can believe anything.

The faults of the radio and of television are less in what they do than what they don't do, or don't do in sufficient amounts and that, in turn, goes back to the fact that only the great mass market can pay enough for radio and television time. Prestige shows of various kinds may be launched, but more people love Lucy than love Toscanini. I don't object to the commercials; they are often very soothing. Their great fault is that they break up the programs too much. I don't want to be told to walk a mile for a Buick or whatever it is when my interest is engaged by a good musical or a good middleweight performance. But I doubt very much if people are put off good music or good reading even by the silliest radio or video programs. They may even be led on to good music, good books (I am using these terms in the old snobbish sense) by inferior programs, by snippets, by an increasing sense of boredom. Nor do I believe that many people, if any, are kept from reading a good book by seeing a version of it on the movies or on television. I don't think Hollywood did any harm to the possible market for *Ivanhoe* or even for *Washington Square* by its versions. Of course, the movies by helping to kill the living theater all over the country have diminished the opportunities for seeing live plays. But a comparison with the theater in Paris and London shows that the debility of the American stage is not solely the fault of the movies.

I am even willing to defend the pocket books that, on their covers at any rate, promise vicarious sexual satisfaction. To put it more accurately, these semibogus works represent a very old tradition. The last volume of one of the most famous of English literary collections, Percy's *Reliques,* is entitled *Lewd, Loose, and Humorous Songs.* It is many years since I studied this valuable work, but if my memory serves me right the first two adjectives, at any rate, were earned. It was a great art collector (but no great reader), Sir Robert Walpole, who announced his dinner party policy at 10 Downing Street and at Houghton, "I always talk bawdy. It's the only thing that everybody is interested in." The publishers of certain paperback books are of the same mind. And so are their readers. This I learn from Freeman Lewis's interesting Bowker lecture, that the most popular of all paper-bound titles is *God's Little Acre.* Erskine Caldwell is a serious author, if not an important one, but it is not for his views on the economic problems of a Southern mill town that millions have bought his book. They took the same interest in it as did the literary editor of a famous British newspaper when he showed me the review copy of the original edition and said (translating into the vernacular), "Get a load of this."

That "skuldudery" (to use Sir Walter Scott's word) is highly marketable is not news, and even if you stick to the classics you don't necessarily escape it. A learned kinsman of mine once assured me that Shakespeare was the dirtiest of English authors if you knew the vocabulary, and while I think not much would be lost if the lurid "powerful" paperbacks disappeared, would the moral tone of the United States be altered for the better?

What is perhaps revealing in the American supply for this universal human demand is the naïveté of the sexuality, the coyness of the illustrations (the Petty girls and the lesser brands of pin-ups). I don't believe that these books and pictures do more than reveal something adolescent about American sexuality. I don't believe they create it. One of Dr. Kinsey's staff might investigate the difference between the American tough novel and the French *roman noir*. The American hero spends most of his time beating, the Frenchman (in works alleged to be *"traduit de l'Américain"*) in bedding. Neither type of book style, taste, or originality does modern American or French culture any credit, but they are by-products, not causes, of whatever weaknesses in American or French society they reveal.

In all the discussions of the cultural level of the mass media, there is (apart from the devotees of the new democratic snobbery) an implied premise that I take to be of very doubtful validity. It is assumed that there was a rich, varied, independent, popular culture which is dead and has been replaced by the mass media of today, mechanically produced and offered to passive, drugged victims of the industrial age. Now, no doubt there were many more independent craftsmen before the coming of modern industry, but there are more ways than one of being a craftsman, and the things we admire most from

Knossos figurines to Limoges enamels were commissioned by rich patrons. Emerson thought or said that the Gothic invaders of the Roman Empire built the cathedrals of the thirteenth century in imitation of their primeval forests. This is no more absurd than in seeing in Chartres the simple, popular expression of a simple faith. It may be that none of the masterpieces, material, musical, or literary, of the past were the work of simple peasants or workers, working to their own taste and needs. It may be that this is the first time that the mass has had any power of command over any but the simplest art forms. And it may be that, left to themselves, the mass of men prefer vulgar, banal, simple works of art.

I do not believe this to be true, but I do not know it to be untrue. "Socialist realism," as the Communist estheticians now call the colored photographs beloved of Stalin, like the music that commissars can hum or whistle, may be what the mass man has always wanted. The mass man need not be a poor man. Squire Western was as barbarous in his tastes as any peasant on his lands. It may be that the kind of literary and musical culture that we of the older school treasure is associated with a class structure that is doomed. It may not be accidental that every important English poet that I can remember, save Shakespeare and Keats, went to Oxford or Cambridge (nearly all to Cambridge, in fact.) Even Shakespeare and Keats got better literary educations than a boy can get (I think) in most American high schools today. Perhaps Cézanne could not have kept on painting if he had not been a rich man. The problem of patronage is a real one. And we must not be surprised if the new mass patron has as simple and gross tastes as Squire Western.

The problem is to make effective the demand of the non-mass patron. As Joseph Wood Krutch has pointed out here, the phonograph has done as much for the improvement of musical taste as the radio, perhaps more, and the interest in high-fidelity recordings, like the increase in the number and proficiency of American amateur musicians and, to me, more surprising, of amateur artists, are signs of grace. For from among the millions of more and more competent performers, listeners, students, may come the first-rate artists. It is possible, too, that we put reading too high as a test of culture. The Anglo-Saxon culture we grew up with has been preeminently a literary culture. Literature has had no rival in prestige like music in Germany and Italy, like painting in France. But music (in France and England as well as in America) is, I think, partly replacing literature, poetry, the drama, the novel as the cultural resource of the minority on whom the burden of maintaining high standards falls. If we think too much in terms of what people read, what plays they see, we may be missing the most important cultural developments of our times.

All the Western countries are going through the double cultural crisis, the crisis caused by industrialism, the crisis caused by democracy. In Europe the severity of the crisis is tempered by nondemocratic survivals, the imperfect equivalents of the old order that forced people to go to churches (many of them not very beautiful), to listen to the liturgy, to read the Bible. In America the crisis is accentuated by the national need to create and impose a general national culture on a people of such diverse origins. This involves creating a new folk culture with very mixed materials. Yet there are possible advantages in the American situation. The first and greatest problems of assimilation are over. America is linguistically and culturally more united than she has been for a century. For good or evil, America is the leader in the making of the new mass culture. If it is made, it will be exported to Western Europe, we may be sure of that, but it will fit America better. It already does and in good ways, for the thinnest American songs, the shoddiest shows are, at any rate, less thin, less shoddy in America than they are when exported.

This is not perhaps a very encouraging judgment. It leaves the masses at the mercy of all the silliest and vulgarest forms of commercialized art. It accepts the possibility that they cannot, in the mass, be rescued from their tastes. But it does not follow (as anxious parents seem to think) that a taste for the comics, for soap opera, for television vaudeville kills or prevents the growth of better taste. Children, boys and girls, can stand a lot of roughage in their intellectual diet. That doesn't matter if they are given more solid food, too. This is a question for the schools, which may be sacrificing the brighter pupils to the mediocrity that offends no susceptibilities, to a "democracy" of taste that means a practically unanimous demand for Grade-B movies. If, as Bentham said, pushpin is as good as poetry if pushpin is what you like, there's no more to be said. But give the boy and girl some chance to sample poetry or its equivalent. Don't be too disappointed if he turns out, like so many eminent lawyers, engineers, linguists, even professors of literature, to have no genuine literary taste. Reading, even the reading of masterpieces, is not the end of life. The schools, the parents, the press all have some remedies in their hands for the degradation of the public taste; so, of course, have the mass media. Prod them, make them ashamed of themselves, but don't expect an Athenian republic with citizens as interested in the results of the play competitions as in the Olympic games. I doubt if even Athens was like that.

And don't forget that we know much more of our own cultural limitations than we do of those of the past. It was a cynical conservative who said that the only result of universal education in England was that rude words were written a foot or so lower down on the walls than they used to be. The boys didn't learn the words any earlier; they only learned to write earlier. Which thing is a parable.

This book has been set in Linotype Caledonia. Designed by W. A. Dwiggins, it is contemporary in two basic respects: it was conceived solely for machine composition, and it does not attempt to reproduce any type of an earlier period. While its ancestors are the so-called transitional types of the eighteenth century, Caledonia is the product of, and is intended for, twentieth-century mass production.

UNIVERSITY OF OKLAHOMA PRESS : NORMAN